FLODDEN

A SCOTTISH TRAGEDY

For Leslie

Peter Reese

FLODDEN

A SCOTTISH TRAGEDY

Birlinn

First published in Great Britain in 2003 by Birlinn Ltd

West Newington House
10 Newington Road
Edinburgh

www.birlinn.co.uk

ISBN 1 84158 265 4

British Library Cataloguing-in-Publication Data
A catalogue record is available on request
from the British Library

Typeset by Palimpsest Book Production Limited,
Polmont, Stirlingshire
Printed and bound by
Creative Print & Design, Ebbw Vale, Wales

CONTENTS

[v]

EPILOGUE:

INTRODUCTION

B EFORE UNDERTAKING THIS book I was quite sure Robert Bruce (Robert I) was Scotland's leading king commander and his triumph at Bannockburn not only Scotland's outstanding victory against the English but self evidently the country's most significant battle from a political standpoint.

Nothing, of course, has changed my mind about the extent of Robert Bruce's achievements nor the merit of his victory at Bannockburn – although if he had been given the opportunity to meet and defeat Edward I there, rather than the English king's inept son, his military reputation would be truly unassailable not only in relation to other Scottish leaders but among military commanders world-wide – but I am no longer convinced about Bannockburn being Scotland's most influential battle.

While Bannockburn undoubtedly laid the foundations for renewed Scottish independence some fourteen years afterwards, England and Scotland were soon fighting again and there were long years of further conflict before Scotland's sovereign status was finally recognised in 1357 through the Treaty of Berwick, an agreement which predictably failed to prevent subsequent English claims to suzerainty. In contrast Scotland's defeat at Flodden served to downgrade the country's military capability and set in train what was to become an irreversible process towards union with England which, despite the recent granting of certain devolved powers, continues today.

Flodden deserves to rate highly amongst Anglo-Scottish battles for other reasons. The number of soldiers engaged there was unquestionably higher than at Bannockburn, higher than in Wallace's battle against the English at Stirling Bridge and even higher than in the massive encounter that took place between the two countries at Pinkie Cleugh in 1547. The one battle where battle numbers were likely to have equalled or exceeded those at Flodden was Wallace's clash with Edward I at Falkirk during 1298. Flodden is also notable for its high numbers of casualties, including a king, many leading nobles and 12,000 or so others killed. These far exceeded the totals at Bannockburn or at Stirling Bridge and stand comparison with the sanguinary encounters of Falkirk and Pinkie, a fact less surprising when one realises its main hand-to-hand engagement was fought with notable stubbornness, and for longer than the others, including William Wallace's primarily defensive engagement against Edward I at Falkirk. And although it was the last medieval engagement fought in Britain due in large part to the obsolescent weapons used by many of the English soldiers, Flodden previsaged more modern battles with its opening artillery engagement.

Whereas every Scottish schoolboy knows of Bannockburn, those I have met recently were less aware of Flodden. Indeed, one needed some persuading I was not referring to Culloden! Understandably Flodden's disastrous results have been deliberately played down in Scotland and, as the book attempts to show, for quite different reasons in England too.

This has had predictable results on its documentation. Whether those responsible for keeping the Scottish records were killed in the conflict or not, there are no contemporary records or accounts of it from north of the border and the major English sources are limited to three. These are the short *Articles of Battle*, likely to have been written by Thomas Howard, Surrey's eldest son and the English vanguard commander; an avowedly contemporary account called the *Trewe Encountre*, which is limited to some few pages: and allusions made to the battle within Edward Hall's *The Triumphant Reigne of Kyng Henry VIII*, printed in 1550 but reputedly based on reports of eye witnesses. Nonetheless, the conjunction of such accounts with contemporary letters and papers, along with later commentaries and a thorough investigation of the ground, has enabled the course of the battle to be traced with some accuracy. This process is made easier because, unlike Bannockburn and Falkirk (1298), the site is in little dispute, and its present memorial undoubtedly marks the location of some of the bitterest fighting. However, the nature of the English approach march, especially the movement of their final division to the battle, remains open to different interpretations.

As in my earlier account of Bannockburn, I attempt to describe the salient political and military developments leading to the conflict, the two armies' different command systems and the use they made of contrasting weaponry, before going on to recount the conflict in detail and assess its important consequences.

On my visits to Branxton field I was struck by the hauntingly beautiful part of Northumberland where the fight occurred, with ruined castles nearby serving to emphasise the bloody history of the border regions as much as the damage inflicted by the Scots during their approach march to Flodden. However, visitors to the battle site are not well served. On my ascents up Piper's Hill I have never failed to meet people puzzling over the simple viewscape there. For further details they are obliged to go to the visitors' centre at Etal Castle over eight kilometres away where principal attention is paid to the castle itself. The time has surely come for a visitor centre to be erected on the battle site – probably near the present car park – where publications can be stocked, an appropriate interactive experience offered, and from where visitors can be directed along a trail to include the approach marches of both armies, the position taken up earlier by the Scots on Flodden Hill and the dispositions and movements of the contenders at Branxton.

ACKNOWLEDGEMENTS

W ITH REGARD TO the book's early stages I am indebted to four people in particular; to Paul Vickers, historian and the army's systems librarian, who walked the battlefield, discussed the conflict's sequence of events and produced the battle maps; to Dr Leslie Wayper, 'historian extraordinaire'; to my long-time friend Mrs Jennifer Prophet for her valued comments on the text and, together with her son Charles, the production of the index, and to Mrs Christine Batten for her ever-skilled work with the computer.

With respect to essential professional support, I have received immense help from, among others, the National Library of Scotland, including its map department, The British Library, Scottish United Services' Museum Library, Royal Armouries Library, Fort Nelson, Edinburgh Central Library, the Army Central Library, Hexham Public Archives, Farnborough Library, from Colonel A. Guinan, T.D. on artillery matters and the Provost and Council of Selkirk at the time of the burgh's annual Common Ridings. For the illustrations I particularly acknowledge the assistance received from the Royal Collection, the National Portrait Gallery, Heinz Archive and Library and the Scottish National Portrait Gallery. The book was written largely in the Prince Consort's Military Library, Aldershot, whose librarian Mr Tim Ward and staff are friends to whom I owe so much over more years than I care to remember.

At Birlinn Books I am, of course, very grateful to Hugh Andrew for his vital endorsement, to Neville Moir for piloting the book through its production stages and to Donald Reid for his rare perception and high editorial skills.

Finally, I am fortunate indeed in the continuing support of my wife who has borne the brunt of my Flodden mania and walked over the special mud of Branxton fields, where in places shoulder high thistles compare well with the best of Scottish ones.

Any errors or deficiencies are, of course, mine alone.

Peter Reese, 2003

LIST OF ILLUSTRATIONS

LIST OF MAPS

PROLOGUE

BURGHMUIR – AUGUST 1513

For he had charged that his array
Should southward march by break of day
Sir Walter Scott, *Marmion*

TWO HUNDRED YEARS after Robert Bruce led his men against King Edward II at Bannockburn another out-standing Scottish king again gathered his nation's host to confront the English.

James IV gave orders for his men to attend on 13 August 1513 'with 40 days provisions'[1] at two assembly points, the Burghmuir (Edinburgh's common moor) to the immediate south of the town, and a forward mustering point at Ellem Kirk in Berwickshire's Duns forest, where he had gathered for his previous foray against Norham Castle in 1497. A good proportion of the men from Lothian, together with those from the north-west, were due to assemble initially at Edinburgh, while those from East Lothian, Fife and Angus would march directly to Ellem,[2] where the whole army was scheduled to meet before moving southwards to the Tweed about twenty miles away. The Edinburgh muster gave James an opportunity to fill the old city with all the panoply of war and show himself in the dual capacity of monarch and military leader, thereby helping him demonstrate the extent of his country's military commitment. Virtually every smith, wheelwright and seamstress would have been enlisted to support the host, the town's bakehouses would have worked continually, while Edinburgh's provost and baillies, after leaving the city's affairs in the hands of their deputies,[3] moved onto the Burghmuir and presented themselves for roll-call.

The muir covered five square miles, with its northernmost

point marked by the Burgh loch lying near the base of the city's walls; its southernmost boundary was the Pow burn. Today the loch that provided Old Edinburgh with drinking water has been drained and transformed into the parkland area of the Meadows, presently surrounded by busy streets, while the burn (now piped and running underground) bounds the city's southernmost districts of West Morningside, Canaan, Blackford, Wester Grange and Mayfield. With such extensive development it is not easy to visualise the Burghmuir of the early sixteenth century, with its unprepossessing air of rough grassland intersected by clumps of ragged and ancient oaks from the one-time forest of Drumselch. King David I had gifted it to the city in 1143, and by the time of Flodden the muir had been used for several purposes: as a haven for outlaws and vagrants who skulked in rough huts or found refuge beneath the trees; as a quarantine area for the city's plague victims; and, in 1384, as the point of assembly for a previous Scottish army reputedly 30,000 strong under the command of the earls of Fife and Douglas.[4] James IV knew the muir well and gave Edinburgh's magistrates the privilege of letting pockets of its land; such grants encouraged the clearing of some of the massive trees, as feu-holders could use the felled timber to extend the frontages of their Edinburgh houses by a maximum of seven feet. This may have helped open out the muir but it came at the cost of reducing the width of Edinburgh's High Street dramatically.

The king had both ridden and hawked on the muir and, in 1507, he established a little chapel dedicated to Saint Roque, the French saint of the plague-stricken, on a site close to the present Astley Ainslie hospital. This chapel, together with the adjacent open ground, became the focus for his muster before Flodden. In his poem *Marmion*, Sir Walter Scott vividly described the likely spectacle of tents 'spread over all the Borough-moor and chequering all the heath between the streamlet (the Pow burn) and the town ... oft giving way where still there stood some relics of the old oak wood.'[5] In the centre of the assembled tents Scott writes:

> The royal banner floated wide,
> The staff a pine tree strong and straight,
> pitched deeply in a massive stone.

The detail may not be authentic – the massive numbers described by Scott were unlikely to have much exceeded 40,000 men (still a large army) and the hole in the present bore stone now cemented into the boundary wall of Morningside parish church, whether the original or not, would not have held any large trunk. Yet Scott's scene, as ever, is compelling:

> The horses' tramp, and tingling clank
> Where chiefs reviewed their vassal rank
> And charger's shrilling neigh;
> And see the shifting lines advance,
> While frequent flash'd from shield and lance,
> The sun's reflected ray.

The bustle and urgency of the assembly was also captured by a reference in the contemporary treasurers' accounts to last-minute embroidery. This was to complete the fringes of the royal standard before the flag could be handed to a horseman who galloped off after sunset to give it to the king.[6] As unit after unit joined the muster, even the more cautious leaders and men must have felt increasingly confident of success, especially as they knew they were yet to meet up with further detachments at Ellem Kirk.

Even more spectacular than the stream of horsemen and foot soldiers hurrying along the town's narrow streets was the rumbling progress of the king's great guns from the castle. These started out on 17 August, two days before the main body left the Burghmuir. The heaviest guns went first but did not get far on the first day; the five great curtals were dragged from the castle to St Mary's Wynd outside the Netherbow Port, where twelve sentries watched over them during the night. On Thursday they resumed their journey; each with its team of thirty-two oxen, their heads swinging and flanks glistening in the rain, probably triple yoked into eight ranks, with more animals roped behind to prevent the carts and their heavy burdens from running away when negotiating the sloping wynds. These were followed two days later by the remaining fifteen guns, accompanied by their own teams of oxen and handlers. In all 400 oxen were needed to pull the guns. Others dragged a crane, pack-horses followed, loaded with shot, both stone and metal, and lastly, after due interval, came a line of carts carrying the vital powder. On Saturday morning the leading infantry units commenced their journey and that evening the king left his palace at Holyrood for the last time to join them.

In spite of widespread support, not everyone shared the king's enthusiasm for the campaign into England. James' veteran adviser, Bishop Elphinstone, spoke openly against it in council and was supported by Archibald Douglas, Earl of Angus. Many other prominent nobles were only too aware of the long and arduous process by which they had reached their present eminence, including both political marriages and shrewd switches of allegiance, and of how much they stood to lose if James were defeated. However, while all were not necessarily over-enthusiastic they duly gave James their support and, apart from Elphinstone and Angus, only the queen made public expression of her concerns about the dangers of such a campaign, especially as the royal succession rested at this time on the uncertain life of their one infant boy, also called James.[7]

In addition to these individual doubts there were reports of two public auguries against the king going to war. The sixteenth-century chronicler, Robert Lindsay of Pitscottie, described how, shortly before the army left the Burghmuir at midnight while some of the artillery was being trundled down from the castle, Robert Lawson, a prominent member of the Lords in Council, heard a raised voice close to the Mercat cross.

This summoned all men, earls, lords, barons, gentlemen and honest burgesses to appear before Plotcok or Pluto (a common name for the devil) within forty days. Lawson appealed against such a mortal threat by calling upon the mercy of God and Jesus Christ, and it would seem his pleas were heard, for of those who were assembling there only Lawson escaped death at Flodden. Pitscottie subsequently qualified his account by acknowledging in his *Historie* that in spite of the information he was given this might just possibly have been a jape mounted by drunks for their amusement.

Pitscottie referred to a second portent, also reported by the renowned sixteenth-century Scottish historian, George Buchanan, who described it as 'a device of the queen and the party averse to the war, to operate on the King's superstition and divert him from his rash projects.'[8] Pitscottie tells that while the king was in Linlithgow praying in church for the success of his expedition, a yellow-haired, balding man, fifty-two years of age, wearing a blue gown and carrying 'ane great pyk staff' in his hand, asked to see the king, and when he had been admitted told him not to lead his army to war and not to use female counsel 'nor lat them twitch they body nor thow thairs'. With this he apparently disappeared, although David Lindsay, later Lyon Herald and Marshal of the royal household, attempted to lay a hand on him.[9] Professor Mackie has suggested that as the king's religious susceptibilities were well-known the figure was most likely to have been an actor dressed to resemble St James.[10] Pitscottie's reference to the further piece of alleged advice, namely that the king should not 'mell' with women, was not taken up by later commentators, although if the actor was, in fact, following the queen's instructions, her indignation over James' mistresses could well have prompted such advice.

The showpiece assembly held by James at the Burghmuir and his forward muster at Ellem Kirk help to confirm other indications that he loved the opportunities for spectacle that attended the reality of war. The very fact that his wife or another of his councillors felt it possible that a suitably devised portent might deter him from his warlike purpose also points to James being a very different war leader from Robert Bruce, who may have been scrupulous in dedicating himself and his men to his maker but had no doubts who shouldered the prime responsibility for their success in battle.

This said, circumstances were more straightforward for Bruce prior to Bannockburn than for James IV before Flodden. As his country's defender Bruce's task was clear, he faced an attack from a massive English army moving into Scotland, if one led by an inept king supported by a divided nobility. In 1513 James himself took the initiative by allying his country to France, and he consciously upped the stakes by assembling his army on France's behalf against a reawakened England under its young king. However warlike James' dreams and colourful his army, his country's interests would not be served by a major battle of attrition, nor, unthinkably, by a serious reverse against the English northern levies.

PART ONE

Rival Kingdoms

CHAPTER ONE

≈

THE DEFENDERS

And much he marvelled one small land,
Could marshal further such various band
Sir Walter Scott, *Marmion*

P ROBLEMS SIMILAR TO those facing James IV as he prepared to cross the border had been experienced by other
Scottish monarchs during the previous four centuries. For in
spite of the Romans' failure to subdue the fierce tribesmen of
the far north and their acceptance of that fact by building the
great barrier wall separating England from what is virtually
modern Scotland, it was not, of course, inevitable that Britain
should remain so divided. That James IV was still king of
an independent Scotland owed as much to generations of its
soldiers as to the statecraft of past kings and their advisers.
Those men who, whatever the dangers or however serious the
defeats, bore arms for their kings and chiefs; men who were
not always well led and had to meet an enemy who, whatever
the calibre of its own leaders, usually possessed both superior
resources and better weaponry.

There were calls to arms from the late eleventh century
onwards for, although much of Europe was still fragmented,
Scotland, under its Canmore line of kings, and England, under
its Saxon and then Norman monarchs, were already distinct
and different countries despite having a border that remained
fluid and created much friction between them. Scotland's
chances of survival against the richer and far more powerful
state to its south were not enhanced by what Scottish historian Ranald Nicholson saw as one of its chief characteristics,
namely that 'Diversity was more obvious than uniformity, local
self-sufficiency more obvious than national inter-dependence.

The concept of one race, one law, one tongue, did not apply in medieval Scotland'.[1] Equally relevant, the writ of Scottish monarchs, including their ability to call out their national host, was traditionally much less pervasive than that exercised by kings in feudal England.[2]

Despite Scotland's greater diversity and looser system of governance, through more than four hundred years, until the union of the two crowns in 1603, Scottish soldiers duelled with their southern adversaries. Sometimes these were mere skirmishes hardly warranting the name of a battle, but at other times they were massive and highly significant engagements, such as Bannockburn or the cataclysmic encounter at Flodden. The reason for such clashes and the nature of their fighting understandably owed much to the prevailing political climate. In this regard three distinct stages can be identified in the ongoing rivalry between the two countries.

The first stretched from the eleventh century until the commencement of the Wars of Independence in the late thirteenth century. This was a time when the English were generally willing to live and let live and the military activity on both sides was relatively unsophisticated. The second was marked by the Wars of Independence from 1286 to 1357 where England was determined to bring about unity by force and Scotland fought for its very existence, with significant strategic and tactical developments taking place on both sides. The third stage ran from the end of the Wars of Independence until the union of the two crowns in 1603.

During the first stage which saw periodic clashes in both countries between the Crowns and their nobility, like that in Scotland following the accession of Alexander I, their external forays tended to be relatively unstructured, with those taking part quite accustomed to changing their allegiance from one side to the other. Frequent marriages took place between the respective royal dynasties, although from time to time England raised its claims of feudal superiority over Scotland

and Scotland showed itself reluctant to give up its claims to the English northern counties. However, like the Romans before them, the English did not give the conquest of the turbulent north a high priority. It did not seem a particularly valuable prize, for the Normans were consolidating their domestic power and had other fish to fry.

When fighting did break out it was more often than not due to Scottish aggression. Such clashes were usually provoked by courtly factions or border disputes and did not amount to serious war. Scottish claims for much of Cumberland and Northumberland were countered by the English belief that the existing border should run on the more northerly Tweed/Cheviot line. Inevitably all military actions in support of Scottish claims meant crossing the English border, and long before James IV Scottish kings came to appreciate the hazards of moving onto English soil. For example, in 1093 when Malcolm III headed an army into England, he was trapped near Alnwick and killed, together with his eldest son.

Fortunately Malcolm had other sons and the reigning English king, William Rufus, was content with sponsoring his favoured candidates from among them for the Scottish throne. Such favour had its costs: the princes came to acknowledge him as their superior, but whether purely for their lands in England or for their possessions further north is not clear. On Rufus' death and the accession of his brother Henry to the English throne, the two crowns edged closer together through the marriage of Henry to Malcolm's III's daughter Edith (whom Henry called Maud). This affiliation was further demonstrated in 1114 after another of Malcolm's sons, Alexander, spent many of his early years at the English court and married Sybilla, daughter of Henry I, before becoming Alexander I of Scotland. After his accession he even accepted joint command of a force campaigning in Wales to establish the English king's overlordship of that country.[3]

The close relationship between the two countries continued

[13]

when Alexander was succeeded by Malcolm's youngest surviving son, David, who was to become one of Scotland's most important early kings. David not only spent much of his boyhood in England, but he gained important holdings there, including the English Honour[4] of Huntingdon (through his marriage to Matilda, widow of Simon de Seulis), and later became Earl of Northampton. As brother-in-law to the English king, he introduced Anglo-Norman families into Scotland, including the Morevilles, Soulis', Lindsays, Somervilles and Bruces, although he did not foresee the problems that would ensue from offering them vast tracts of land in a country where their chances of gaining high influence appeared more favourable than in England.

As a rapid dividend such armoured knights and their followers helped to bolster his crown against its Scottish challengers, and after 1130 also helped to subdue a rebellion in Moray, as well as joining his invasion of Northumberland in furtherance of his claims there. Despite their help, however, David, like so many other Scottish kings, over-stretched himself whilst on English soil. In 1138 near Northallerton, at the so-called Battle of the Standard, the English fought round a mast bearing a consecrated host accompanied by the holy banners of St Peter of York, St John of Beverley and St Wilfred of Ripon, and David's impulsive, lightly armed Galwegians broke against a force of dismounted mailed knights interspersed with archers. This tactical formation was designed to protect the mast, but in future years various versions of it would lead to notable English battlefield successes. In spite of his defeat, David believed he still had a good chance of receiving most of Northumberland when his friend, Henry of Anjou, became king of England, but the new English king not only reneged on his earlier promise but forced David's successor Malcolm IV of Scotland to give up any such claims.

In 1173, once again in the hope of gaining land from the English northern counties, David's grandson, William the Lyon, led an army in support of a rebellion mounted by

Henry II's son against his father. William's campaign, like others during this period, was lacking in strategic planning and battlefield control. Intent upon devastation and plunder, William left part of his army in the west and took the remainder, including Norman knights with estates in Scotland and a band of Flemish mercenaries, to besiege the English border town of Alnwick. Under cover of mist an English force succeeded in capturing him and in punishment Henry II made William his vassal 'for both Scotland and all his other lands'; the subsequent treaty of Falaise (1174) declaring that English lordship extended over Scotland and not just William's English estates. By the treaty William also had to surrender his five strongest castles and to make both his bishops and lay barons subject to the English king. However, although William's rashness encouraged the English crown to bring Scotland more closely under its control, it also gave rise to a mounting sense of national identity within Scotland itself against such alien dominance. Henry attempted to speed the process of assimilation by offering his own granddaughter to William in marriage and, when this was rejected by the Pope on grounds of consanguinity, substituted Ermengarde, the daughter of one of his senior barons and great-granddaughter of Henry I. As her dowry he even returned Edinburgh to William.

It is possible that, under Henry I, England and Scotland might have merged, even before England succeeded in subduing Wales, but Henry's policy was not followed by his successor, Richard I. Arguably England's greatest warrior king, he could, in all probability, have conquered Scotland long before Edward I managed it. But Richard preferred to do his fighting on crusade in the Holy Land using England as his milch-cow to provide the money to do so. Willing as he was to put England's interests for sale, it is not surprising he sold the pass in Scotland, too, although the price he set for the Scottish king's release was not low, particularly for a poor country, with the ransom being fixed at 10,000 marks (£6600).

[15]

Understandably relations between the two countries deteriorated when, with King John on the English throne, William
the Lyon revived his earlier demands for Northumberland and
Cumberland. Both countries prepared for war, but when, in
August 1209, John approached the border castle of Norham
with a much superior army the ageing Scottish king surrendered without a fight. He was forced to pay 15,000 marks
(even more than his earlier ransom) for John's goodwill and to
deliver his two daughters into the English king's custody, on the
understanding that they would marry English rather than
French or other European princes. For more than fifty years
William the Lyon had taken startling military risks, unjustifiable in national terms, to acquire Northumberland.

Following his death, England and Scotland began to draw
together again. The Lyon's young son, who became Alexander
II, had frequently resided at the English court and in 1216
he was among those who greeted the French king when he
landed at Dover. However, King John's troubles with his
barons and the struggle that led to the signing of Magna
Carta in 1215 were too strong a temptation for Alexander to
resist and he joined forces with the English barons, bringing
upon himself an attack by the English army which almost
annihilated his forces.

Close ties between the two royal houses were restored
when in 1221 Alexander II married Joan, daughter of King
John, and in 1237 Scotland finally dropped its claim to
Northumberland and Cumberland in return for a token
income from lands in the two counties to the value of
just £200.[5] The policy of intermarriage continued when
Alexander III, while still a minor, married Henry III's daughter
Margaret. However, such a long-term strategy of integration
through marriage could never satisfy England's next king,
Margaret's impatient and formidable brother Edward I, who
aimed to bring both Wales and Scotland under England's
control during his lifetime.

*　　*　　*

Edward not only wanted to subjugate Scotland but he was willing to use whatever military means he felt necessary to achieve it, and his accession marked the second stage in the ongoing political and military rivalry between the two countries.

For a brief period it seemed as if Edward's ambitions towards Scotland might be achieved peacefully. When Alexander III was accidentally killed in 1286, leaving as sole survivor of the Canmore line his granddaughter, the Maid of Norway, Edward at once proposed that she should marry his son and heir, the seven-year-old Prince Edward Caernarvon. But with the maid's death in 1291 and Edward's continuing determination to pursue his aims towards Scotland, war became inevitable.

When in 1296 Edward made his first attempt to coerce Scotland he massacred both soldiers and civilians in the Scottish border fortress of Berwick, thereby signalling that the fighting would be both bitter and bloody and marked by large and costly battles. In 1297 William Wallace responded with a notable success at Stirling Bridge where he prevented Edward's lieutenant, Warenne, Earl of Surrey, using his full strength, only for this to be followed the next year by Edward's revenge when the English main army gained an overwhelming victory over Wallace at Falkirk. Following Falkirk, Edward pursued Wallace relentlessly until taking a terrible revenge on him in 1305. The mood of the time was also reflected in the implacable attitude adopted by Edward against the rebellious Robert Bruce, who had declared himself King of Scotland. The English king ordered his commander Aymer de Valence to seek out and destroy Bruce, and he authorised Valence to ride under the dragon banner, which enabled him to declare Bruce and his followers outlaws and therefore subject them to the dire punishments of the day.

Nor was savagery confined to one side. After his victory at Stirling Bridge, Wallace flayed the body of Cressingham, the dead English vanguard commander, and sent the skin across Scotland as proof of his victory. In his turn Robert Bruce killed his leading Scottish rival, John Comyn, on the steps of the great altar of Dumfries parish church, while his subsequent harrying of the Buchan estates following his victory at Inverurie in 1308 caused men to grieve there for fifty years afterwards.[6] In such a climate the earlier chivalric sallies were a thing of the past.

The intensity and duration of this conflict brought new military developments. Following William Wallace's defeat at Falkirk, Robert Bruce adopted the classic survival policy of devastating his own country and exchanging ground for time until, hopefully, the English invaders lost momentum. He combined this with guerrilla warfare, in other words avoiding large clashes unless the conditions were strongly in his favour, a doctrine that became known as Good King Robert's Testament, and included the capture, and then destruction, of castle strongholds to deprive the English army of possible bases. Bruce also developed the defensive battlefield formations of massed spearmen instigated by William Wallace into mobile units that owed much to the Swiss halberdiers or ancient Greek phalanxes, and which, in Bruce's hands, were used at Bannockburn (1314) to devastating effect. Unfortunately, in those of later and lesser commanders this formation was to cast a bloody shadow over Scottish military fortunes when they ignored the fact that, although, at Bannockburn, Bruce defeated the unsupported cavalry of a maladroit Edward II, his doctrine was essentially one of caution and manoeuvre. It was lack of a close combination of cavalry, spearmen and archers that had cost the English so dear at Bannockburn, but they learned from their defeat there, and the same cavalrymen who had thundered around aimlessly on that field came to fight dismounted with their spearmen, protected by covering fire from bowmen stationed on their flanks. This combination would long confound the Scots and also succeed against the French in battles such as Crécy and Poitiers in 1356.

As invaders, the English also sought to develop ways of striking deep into the Scottish heartland, and if they were unable to trap the Scottish main army they looked to take over castle strongholds to help consolidate and prolong their presence. These gave rise to new logistical developments: they began to use ships to help their resupply, like those which docked at Leith to restock Edward II's army just prior to Bannockburn, as well as prefabricated pontoon bridges to cross the great river barriers in order to speed their penetration into central Scotland. Additionally, to keep his soldiers in the field for the relatively long periods needed, Edward I also began to pay his regular retinues as well as foreign mercenaries.[7] Such initiatives placed a crushing burden on the English exchequer for, in addition to his soldiers' wages, after capturing the castle strongholds Edward needed to rebuild and garrison them until Scottish resistance could be extinguished.

The fact remains, however, that during the first War of Independence Scotland not only demonstrated formidable powers of resistance but, under Robert Bruce's leadership, established a degree of military superiority that prevented the more powerful southern state from subduing the country until in 1328, after thirty-four years of fighting, the English were forced to discuss peace terms. Following Bannockburn a series of fruitless campaigns left the English forces demoralised and, with their treasury temporarily bankrupted they were no longer able to protect their northern counties from Bruce's well-orchestrated invasions. For Scottish arms this represented a staggering achievement, for England a humiliating defeat; nothing less could have brought the English to the conference table.

By the Treaty of Northampton England recognised that Bruce and his heirs should be free of any English feudal claims and Scotland should also be both free and distinct from England; both sides agreed to underscore the agreement with a royal marriage, this time between Prince David of Scotland and Edward III's sister Joan. In his desire for peace Robert Bruce also agreed to pay an indemnity of £20,000 within three years. He still, however, retained his defence agreement with France which in itself was bound to make England feel partly encircled. More serious still, the Scottish king did virtually nothing for the 'disinherited', the group of militant nobles who by the agreement lost both their lands and their titles. Robert Bruce had been forced to crush the factions within Scotland before he could take on the English, and with his own early changes of allegiance he knew only too well the problems of conflicting loyalties. The treaty therefore specified that those with lands in Scotland who did not become Scottish would lose their holdings. However, in the vast majority of cases he offered no compensation for such lost estates, nor made any redistribution of land in their favour.[8]

With influential men from both sides of the border determined to regain their lands, and a proud young king on the English throne intent on avenging his humiliation in battle against the Scots, an early resumption of hostilities was inevitable. Within a year Edward III renewed English attempts to subjugate Scotland, and this second half of the so-called Wars of Independence was to continue for a further twenty-seven years, during which time relations between the two states fell to their earlier abysmal levels and the Scots were again forced to refuse open battle until time worked to their advantage. As Bruce had feared, while English leadership grew in vigour and English tactics evolved significantly, leadership slackened in the northern kingdom. The king died in 1329 leaving a son just four years old; a short time later, with the death of Thomas Randolph, Earl of Moray, the last of his famous commanders had gone, too. With them went any full appreciation of the war's earlier lessons.

Edward III began by giving covert help to the disinherited, enabling them to assemble a small army, less than 3000 strong but mainly made up of archers, whom the English king allowed to sail to Scotland in eighty-eight ships. This was jointly commanded by Henry Beaumont, Earl of Buchan, and Edward Balliol, son of the Scottish king usurped by Robert Bruce, whom Beaumont persuaded to come over from France to claim 'his rightful inheritance'. On 11 August 1332 at

Dupplin Moor near Perth, they defeated a much larger, if dangerously over-confident, Scottish force, led by their newly appointed guardian, Donald of Mar. At Dupplin Scottish leadership lost virtually all tactical control following a public quarrel between Mar and Sir Robert Bruce (Bruce's bastard son), and their attacking schiltrons were cut to pieces by an English formation of dismounted men-at-arms supported by longbowmen on their flanks.[9]

Following his victory Edward Balliol was crowned at Scone, where Bruce's young son, David II, had been both crowned and anointed the year before. Yet, however much the death of Robert Bruce and the succession of his four-year-old son weakened Scottish fighting ability, the majority of Scottish nobles were not prepared to support the regime of a man who was so obviously the English king's puppet. In December Balliol's small force was attacked and he fled to Carlisle, where he once again appealed to Edward III for help. Although Balliol had already paid homage to the English king for such support he now additionally pledged Berwick to him, together with areas of land equivalent to a massive 2000 librates[10] covering much of southern Scotland.

In March 1333, supported by a strong English force, Balliol duly re-crossed the border and besieged Berwick; the official resumption of war between England and Scotland came two months later when Edward III joined in the siege. Edward was subsequently to prove an even better commander than his grandfather and, with no adequate substitutes for Bruce's renowned commanders, further Scottish misfortunes were all too likely. Mar was succeeded by Andrew Moray, son of Bruce's great captain and a capable soldier, but he was captured in October 1332 and subsequently imprisoned in England, to be replaced by Archibald Douglas, a younger brother of Bruce's great captain, but with hardly anything of his brother's military talent.

As Berwick was due to surrender by 20 July 1333 the Scots faced the same problem as the English at Bannockburn, namely the need to relieve a fortress. On 19 July Douglas moved to confront the army that Edward had placed on Halidon Hill, a feature some two miles north-west of Berwick dominating the port's landward approaches. To reach his opponents Douglas had to cross marshy ground before climbing the hill's most accessible northern slope on the crest of which stood three divisions of dismounted English knights and men-at-arms, each protected by flanking archers placed in wedge-shaped formations. At Dupplin Moor this combination had already served Balliol well but at Halidon Hill it caused the Scots to fight one of their most disadvantageous battles. Among the high number of Scottish casualties was another guardian and five Scottish earls.

Berwick fell to the English the next day and Edward I's savagery during the first War of Independence was repeated when his grandson ordered the prisoners to be executed. Edward III intended to put the whole country under the control of his lackey Edward Balliol; he was confident its subjection was close, because with the number of casualties already suffered, he believed it would no longer have the 'capacity, knowledge, or desire to assemble a (further) fighting force or to command it had it been assembled.'[11] Balliol was left to complete the conquest but, like his grandfather, Edward III badly underestimated the Scottish powers of determination and resistance, with or without French help, and he was even less willing than Edward I to commit the vast resources needed to hold on to the annexed areas.

Meanwhile the Scots refound the commander they needed when, during the summer of 1334, Andrew Moray was ransomed from English capacity and reappointed guardian. They turned to the offensive and overran much of southwest Scotland, causing dissension among the disinherited and forcing Edward Balliol once again to flee across the border. This led Edward himself to mount a series of campaigns reminiscent of the earlier wars, aimed at suppressing an obstinate and dogged enemy. He soon came to appreciate the extent of his task when, in November 1334, he embarked upon a winter campaign, the sole achievement of which was the repair and garrisoning of Roxburgh Castle.

Back in London French diplomatic pressure brought about a truce between England and Scotland until midsummer 1335, an interval which Edward used to prepare for yet another Scottish invasion. This followed the pattern of his grandfather's thirty years before, and employed a force similar in size to that which he would assemble for his campaign in France the following year. As Edward moved deep into Scotland, his hopes that more Scottish magnates would join him proved correct, and among those who deserted the nationalist cause were the earls of Fife and Mentieth and even Robert Stewart, future king of Scotland.

In spite of such prominent turncoats, however, the methods used by the English to subdue Scotland denied them popular support. Edward Balliol, for instance, chose one of the disinherited, David Strathbogie, Earl of Atholl, as his lieutenant in northern Scotland. The chronicler, John of Fordun, described his bloody revenge against Bruce's supporters: 'Some he disinherited, others he murdered; and in the end, he cast in his mind how he might wipe out the Freeholders from the face of the earth.'[12] The crowning point of Strathbogie's campaign was his siege of Kildrummy Castle which was held by Andrew Moray's wife, Christiana Bruce, sister of the late king. But in November 1335 his 3000-strong army was defeated in the forest of Culbean, close to the castle, by 800 men under Andrew Moray, aided by the Earl of March and William Douglas. While a relatively small success, it ended the sequence of Scottish defeats and gave the defenders new heart to reverse most of Edward's gains during his great summer offensive.

Moray faced his sternest test as military leader during Edward III's offensives in 1336 and 1337, when the English king began erecting or repairing castle strongholds with the aim of dominating Scotland. The success of this strategy, however, as with Hitler's during his invasion of Russia nearly

600 years later, was jeopardised by the ruthless conduct of the officials who followed the soldiers, and the wholesale forfeitures of freehold properties made the Balliol administration thoroughly hated.

By 1337, like his grandfather and father before him, Edward III was compelled to realise the difficulties involved in conquering Scotland: the costs of mounting northern campaigns were not only crippling but the returns that could be extracted from devastated tracts of land proved disappointing.[13] In any event, France appeared to offer not only greater glories but far better material rewards and, in addition, by defeating France Edward could weaken Scotland by removing its habitual ally. France's alignment with Scotland (and its threat to send troops in active support) played its part in encouraging Edward to invade, thus beginning the costly and seemingly endless Hundred Years War, which was to last – with truces – until 1453.

With Edward away, the Scots under Moray steadily won back English strongholds in the south and, even after Moray's death in 1338, this process continued until by 1342 all except Berwick had been recaptured. It now seemed feasible to consider counter measures in the shape of raids on the English northern counties, and further encouragement came in the summer of 1341 with the return of Scotland's king after his seven-year refuge in France. Now seventeen, David II took part in sizeable forays across the border during 1342, 1345 and 1346 before, in response to an appeal from the French, gathering together in October 1346 an army larger than at any time since Halidon Hill.

While the English had failed to conquer Scotland David II, like other Scottish kings before him, was to discover how dangerous it was to move into the English border counties with their efficient system of mobilisation. The Scottish army, commanded by a leader who so far had shown little of his father's military talents, was brought to battle at Neville's Cross outside Durham. There the formidable combination of English men-at-arms supported by archers on their flanks once again prevailed against brave but poorly co-ordinated attacks. Many Scottish magnates were killed but worst of all the Scottish king was captured. For the Scots it was Halidon Hill again, with the added penalty of having their king fall into enemy hands, but there was the unquestionable bonus that, in order to maximise David II's capture, Edward was obliged to recognise him and the Stewart line, rather than Edward Balliol, as the true kings of Scotland. Predictably, the immediate result of Neville's Cross came in 1347 when an expedition led by Edward Balliol reversed most of the earlier Scottish gains the previous year. However, the cream of England's soldiers were with their king in France and consequently the unfortunate Balliol was too weak to garrison the territories he had won.

Negotiations over the release of David II continued for eleven years, but by now the Scots were refusing to jeopardise their independence in return for the release of their king, and 'any proposal that implied future English overlordship was emphatically rejected.'[14] Initially Edward III's demands were high and, in 1355, in response to new French appeals but also in the hope of reducing such demands, the Scots besieged Berwick Castle. This brought the English king back from France and in 1356, still styling himself king of Scotland (as well as of England and France), he embarked on what was to be his last expedition northwards. It was a destructive if indeterminate campaign that was given the wry title of 'the Burnt Candlemas', but through a shortage of supplies his army was compelled to pull back. Edward then returned to France where he was far more successful and, after the great English victory at Poitiers in September of the next year, Scotland realised it must reopen serious negotiations for its king's release. A ransom of 100,000 marks (£67,000) was agreed, to be paid in ten instalments during which time both sides would be under truce and normal trade links could be re-opened. On 7 October 1357 king David II returned to his kingdom a free man; with his homecoming Edward Balliol's regal hopes died and the long civil war between the

Comyn faction (supported by the English) and the Bruces was over.

Edward III was fought out as far as Scotland was concerned, his attempts to conquer the country having proven unsuccessful. With his soldierly talents and the support of magnificent English longbowmen he could beat the Scots in battle, especially when their leadership proved disunited or over-confident; but, despite massive English expenditure, when their soldiers refused battle against the English main army and made full use of their country's defensive features, like Vietnam in the twentieth century confronting vast American technological predominance, Scotland proved virtually unconquerable.

The deaths of both Edward III and David II during the later years of the fourteenth century heralded the opening of the third stage in the military rivalry between the two countries. This was marked by prolonged and difficult struggles in both countries to establish their regal supremacy until the sixteenth century saw a return to large scale battles. From the 1350s high mortality and wastage caused by the plague struck both England and Scotland while, for the best part of 100 years, England's soldiers were heavily committed in France. Widespread domestic discord also affected both countries. During the Wars of the Roses in England rival contenders for the throne, accompanied by their armies of retainers, fought for primacy. In Scotland, where the centralisation of power was still at an earlier stage, the crown not only suffered from recurrent minorities but, until the end of the fifteenth century, failed to assert itself fully against a powerful baronage of half-tribal, half-feudal lords.

As a result military engagements between them tended to be restricted, with the Scots seeking to regain their castles still left in English hands and the English tending to react most strongly against any Scottish interference in their domestic quarrels or to possible French involvement in the northern kingdom.

In Scotland towards the end of the fourteenth century David II had been succeeded by two relatively unimpressive kings, Robert II and Robert III, who allowed great marcher lords like the Douglases to fight the English Percies and to assume the sweeping powers required to finance their seemingly unending clashes, albeit ones confined to the border regions. However, from 1406 onwards, when the first three Jameses came to the throne, they showed themselves anxious to restore the power of a sovereign Scotland, by suborning their nobles while trying to find ways of recovering the Scottish border castles still in English hands. As the Scottish magnates at this time were extremely powerful and, like the Clan Donald in the north-west and the islands, exercised an authority almost independent of the king, the contest promised to be hard and long, leaving relatively little opportunity for centrally co-ordinated initiatives against England

At the opening of the fifteenth century, for instance, the Scottish reverse at Homildon Hill gave the English strong reasons for doubting that country's ability to mount any worthwhile military challenge. Following earlier border clashes attempts were made to end Scottish technical inferiority by increasing their proportion of archers and providing plate armour to better protect their spearmen against the English longbows. However, after a large Scottish force raided northern England in 1402 in retaliation for a previous reverse suffered at Nesbit Muir, it was caught at Homildon Hill close to the border by Harry Percy (Hotspur), son of the Earl of Northumberland, accompanied by the renegade – but able – Scottish commander, the Earl of March. At Homildon English longbows prevailed once more: the chronicler Bower graphically described their arrows tearing into the massed Scottish ranks and 'transfixing the hands and arms of the Scots to their lances.'[15] After a stubborn and bloody engagement the Scots finally had to give way, to be pursued to the Tweed some thirteen miles to the north. The earlier (and lesser) Scottish defeat of Hotspur at Otterburn in 1388 had been avenged;

thousands of men reputedly died at Homildon and five hundred were drowned in the Tweed, while many Scottish nobles were made prisoners, including Archibald, Earl of Douglas. Homildon represented a defeat on the scale of earlier setbacks at Dupplin, Halidon and Neville's Cross during the Wars of Independence, and although the English showed no intention of following up their success it undoubtedly influenced the cautious military stance adopted by James I where England was concerned.

It was, in fact, many years before James I was able to exert his royal powers. Just before his father's death he was captured by pirates as he was crossing to France and delivered to the English king, as a result of which he was compelled to spend the next eighteen years in captivity. Significantly, the English appeared to view the possession of James and the other influential prisoners taken at Homildon less as a means of attempting to crush Scotland than a way of keeping the border regions quiet while concentrating on their main war with France. James did not return to Scotland until 1424; in the intervening period he married Henry V's cousin, Joan Beaufort, and acquired the accomplishments of an English prince[16] as well as becoming familiar with the English theory and practice of royal government. The Scots agreed to pay 50,000 marks on his release and hand over other specified hostages, but the English did not succeed in their further aim – one that showed where their priorities lay – of bringing about the recall of the highly rated Scottish soldiers who were then fighting voluntarily against them in France.

When James I assumed power in 1424, his energy and determination quickly became evident. His admirer, Walter Bower, abbot of Inchcolm, writing a decade after James' death, described his wide range of accomplishments, including archery, hand tennis and gaming at tables, and pointed to the king's knowledge of scripture, poetic composition and music. Far more important than any such evidence of English courtly skills, however, was his appetite for using and, most significantly, enhancing his regal authority, since there was the pressing need for him to restore order and peace within his unruly kingdom. Bower describes James pledging himself to see that all subjects could feel themselves treated justly: 'If God spares me; gives me help and offers me at least the life of a dog; I shall see to it throughout my kingdom that the key . . . guards the castle and the thorn bushes the cow.'[17]

It was a hard task, for, as his biographer, Dr Michael Brown, graphically points out, he returned to a Scotland where the royal name of Stewart probably carried less credit than that of Douglas.[18] But by 1437 the first James had succeeded in changing this, and in little more than a year he destroyed the power of the Albany Stewarts who had dominated Scottish politics for a generation.

His determination to assert his rule over the nobles who had become so powerful in his absence never faltered. During his captivity James had closely watched the conduct of Henry V, then at the height of his powers, and had noted his exercise of central authority, and however adverse his initial position vis-à-vis the magnates, he clearly attempted to model himself upon the English king. He destroyed some of the powerful magnates, most notably Murdac, Duke of Albany, and threatened many more. Seemingly insensitive to the protests of those he impoverished he succeeded in not only accumulating the crown's wealth but in doubling its royal land holdings. In his later years this enabled him to live a life of great luxury: in addition to using Edinburgh, Perth and Stirling as the revolving seats of his royal court, he lavished £3,000 on Linlithgow Palace, the traditional staging-post between Edinburgh and Stirling. Between 1428 and 1434 his expenditure on this single building project represented over a tenth of his annual income.[19]

In external relations James I was cautious but astute, taking advantage of an England embroiled with France by procrastinating over payments for his ransom, until by 1436 he was negotiating for the peaceful return, of Roxburgh and

Berwick in exchange for his greater co-operation. At the same time he found himself courted by France which, after suffering several heavy defeats at English hands, pressed him to renew their countries' past treaties of mutual support. For eight years he skilfully prevaricated before sending his daughter Margaret to marry the French dauphin. This committed Scotland to the French camp and soon there were predictable and pressing requests for military action against England; James' modest response was to mount an attack on Roxburgh Castle, much the smaller of the last two English strongholds in Scotland.

Whatever political skills James had acquired from Henry V he also witnessed English methods of war fighting. He had taken part in their French campaigns and at the siege of Dreux in 1421 had watched cannon being used. This convinced him that here was a genuinely new weapon of war and, more important still, one uniquely equipped to meet the requirements of his own country. Accordingly he purchased – at great cost – heavy cannon from Flanders that were operated by German gunners under the command of Johannes Paule, whom James grandly termed 'master of the King's engines'. James developed what can only be described as an intense interest in some of his pieces, including one that Walter Bower described as 'a great brass bombard' which carried an inscription on its barrel, 'For the illustrious James . . . I was made at his order, therefore I am called Lion.'[20] Cannon meant that a Scottish force, in the initial stages at least, could fight an engagement at a distance beyond the range of English longbowmen.

James, confident his artillery train would quickly batter down the walls of Roxburgh Castle, gathered a formidable host, including a significant proportion of archers who were expected to work directly with the new arm. But to his disappointment the garrison at Roxburgh resisted determinedly and after fourteen days a strong English force arrived to lift the siege. When James learned of their approach he abandoned his positions in such haste that he was forced to leave his prized artillery behind, a move that proved a massive blow to his personal prestige, and much weakened him, but in his defence heavy cannon was immensely difficult to move at this time.

A bare six months following his humiliation before Roxburgh, James managed to alienate most of the powerful Scottish nobles in his attempt to extend his personal power and, more culpably, he neglected to ensure the loyalty of his own officers of state and the trust of his military commanders. He was assassinated on 20 February 1437 among members of his own household.

James I's murder put a brake on the attempts of the Scottish monarchs both to reassert their authority and develop their war-fighting ability. On his death his six-year-old son came to the throne and within a month he was crowned as James II in the palace of Holyrood, possibly due to fears for his personal safety if he ventured to Scone. Such fears seemed legitimate for, after his father's murderers had been caught and executed, there was, during his long minority, much manoeuvring among the nobility to seize the levers of power; indeed, while James was riding near Stirling in 1439 he was abducted by Sir Alexander Livingston and Sir William Crichton.

When James was finally able to assume his royal power he – like his father – determined to elevate his royal office within Scotland and it is therefore unsurprising that his first major action in 1450 was to move against the powerful Livingston family. Their lands were forfeited and the younger Alexander Livingston (constable of Stirling Castle) and Robert Livingston were executed; understandably William, Lord Crichton, was quick to offer very substantial loans to assist the king with his immediate financial problems.[21]

Powerful as they became, the Livingstons and Crichtons could never compare with the Douglases and the king swiftly moved on to meet the greater challenge. While the head of the family, William, 8th Earl of Douglas, was in Rome, James raised charges against both him and his family. In February 1452 discussions on these and other contentious matters were held at Stirling Castle where, on the second day, the king fell into a rage and stabbed Douglas to death. Although the Douglases attempted to challenge the murder, James II responded (in a more subtle way than his father would have done) by convening a parliament which, albeit uneasily, gave him its support. Armed with such assurance, by 1455 the king felt strong enough to launch further attacks on both the Douglases and the Hamiltons: the Hamiltons rapidly submitted and after the Douglases were formally forfeited by parliament James moved to attack their strongholds.

In military terms, like his father, James proved an enthusiast for cannon and so expanded his train that by 1458 he had appointed a master of artillery in the person of one William Bonar.[22] His heavy cannon included Mons Meg, the famous bombard given him by the Duke of Burgundy, which, together with other pieces, had been escorted on its journey to Scotland by fifty men-at-arms. Unlike Roxburgh when attacked by James I, the Douglas castles had no relieving force, without which they were soon battered into submission. Eventually their only major stronghold was the reputedly impregnable fortress of Threave Castle in Galloway, which stood on its own island. James was personally involved in besieging it and after a sustained bombardment lasting some weeks the garrison surrendered. The only sanctuary remaining for the once all-powerful William Douglas was England.

These successes gave James II his wish for additional wealth, and more important still, increased royal prestige, but unlike his father he was also careful to reward the subjects who proved loyal to him, making, for instance, Colin, Lord Campbell, Earl of Argyll.

Although the historian John Major rated James I over both his son and grandson, he acknowledged that 'most writers give the first place to this monarch [James II] seeing that he gave himself with all zeal to the things of war and to naught else.'[23] James II's emphasis on his country's preparedness was seen in the acts of parliament passed for regular 'wappenshaws' to be held, where weapons and equipment could be inspected, and where archery could be favoured over such time-wasting pursuits as football and golf that were to be 'cryit downe and nocht usyt'. Such directives were fully in accord with those of his father's parliaments who, 'forbiddis that no man play at the fut ball and if they persisted fining them four-pence.'[24]

It was, of course, one thing attacking rebellious Douglases who had no artillery, quite another to consider moving against the English, and when he did so the scale of his operations was, like his father's, undoubtedly modest. Although the two countries were at truce he diverted part of the army he had set down before Threave in order to mount a surprise attack on Berwick, where Douglas himself was likely to have taken refuge. The confused situation in England following the defeat of the Lancastrians at the Battle of St Albans in May 1455 hampered the relief, and James attempted to increase English difficulties by asking Charles VII of France to mount a simultaneous attack on Calais.[25] Charles refused, pleading other difficulties, and James was forced to call off his attack because the Berwick defences were too strong, but the next year he raided the lands controlled by the English garrison at Roxburgh and managed to acquire some booty. Despite his enthusiasm for things military, however, James II did not prove an outstanding commander: his attack on the Isle of Man, guarded by the English Stanley family, was on too small a scale, and after it had failed the Stanleys, in reprisal, raided Kirkcudbright, burning and plundering the town. James had hoped to make a further attack on Berwick during 1457 but the improvement in its defences made this impractical. Two years earlier, during a parliament at Stirling, James II had acts passed for the better defence of the borders, but these authorised just 400 soldiers to garrison the vulnerable East March opposite Berwick, which could hardly compare with English arrangements that allotted £2000 sterling for the defence of Roxburgh alone, a figure ranging from a third to a half of the Scottish king's normal annual income.[26] Such a disparity between the two countries' resources certainly justified Norman MacDougall's conclusion – made with regard to James III – that 'the lesson for the Scots king was clear; short of a total government collapse in England, or the unlikely possibility of French military assistance, raids on English controlled territory on the Borders or Man were a very dangerous game to play, inviting immediate and devastating retaliation.'[27] It would still be a dangerous initiative in 1513.

On 10 July 1460, however, a rare opportunity appeared for the Scottish king when a Yorkist victory over the Lancastrians at the Battle of Northampton marked the start of outright civil war in England. James had been watching events carefully and must have made preliminary arrangements, for he succeeded in mustering his army, complete with its heavy guns, within fourteen days. By the end of July, with forces drawn from right across Scotland, he laid siege to Roxburgh, the castle that had defied his father's attack, justifiably confident in his formidable artillery train following its performance against Threave Castle. The ordnance of the day was not reliable, however, and James, who insisted on closely supervising its firing, was fatally injured when a gun disintegrated and severed his thigh bone.[28]

The substitution of a vigorous, 29-year-old king by an eight-year-old child (crowned as James III at Kelso Abbey a week after his father's death) brought fresh and unexpected dangers to the Scottish crown. The chronicler Auchinleck could understandably talk of the 'Gret Dolour' felt throughout the country (not, though it must be acknowledged, among all the nobles), but such had been the personality of the dead king that at Roxburgh 'all the lordis that war thar remanit still with the ost and on the Friday efter richt wysly and manfully want the forsaid castell.'[29] After capturing Roxburgh Castle they went on to destroy it but, as a result of James' death, Berwick, the last fortress occupied by the English, remained unscathed.

[34]

The next James has been described by his biographer, Norman MacDougall, as 'a disaster in personal and public life alike'[30] and he was indeed much the least successful of the first three Stewart kings. In all James III reigned twenty-eight years, but during the period of his minority state affairs were conducted by different factions, for the initial nine years by his pro-Yorkist mother, Mary of Gueldres, then by the Lancastrian supporter, Bishop James Kennedy, and finally, during the last four years before he assumed power, by the Boyds.

At that time England was experiencing grave problems of its own and in 1461 Scotland finally succeeded in regaining Berwick, although not by force of arms. The fortress was surrendered by Margaret of Anjou, queen of Henry VI, in return for asylum being granted to her in Scotland. Following prolonged negotiations after the Yorkist Edward IV seized the English throne, the Scots finally returned Henry VI to England and a truce was agreed. During his supervision of the crown Thomas Boyd married the king's sister and, after being created Earl of Arran, took upon himself the responsibility of marrying the sixteen-year-old king to Margaret, daughter of Christian I of Norway, a match that promised to bring with it the advantageous pledge for Orkney and Shetland to become part of Scotland. Arran, though, did not receive the credit he might have expected: immediately after his marriage James III used his royal powers to have the Boyds attainted for many crimes, most notably for 'taking upon themselves the rule and governance of our person and our brothers.'[31]

The king soon made his mark on foreign policy for, contrary to the first two Jameses, he actively sought an alliance with England, and in 1473 a match was agreed between James' son, born in March of that year, and Edward IV's daughter, who was three years older. The betrothal was celebrated at Greyfriars Church in Edinburgh and the English, who at the time were planning to invade France and needed an ally on their northern border, agreed to pay 2000 marks towards a full dowry of

20,000 marks. In the following year a treaty of perpetual peace was duly concluded between the two countries. A continuing peace between such long-standing adversaries was beyond the imagination of many on either side, but James went on to seek friendship with England throughout his reign.

In such circumstances he was not likely to spend heavily on military forces, particularly as he was miserly and loved to hoard his money in large black chests, rather than spending it in such traditional ways as the building or refurbishment of the royal palaces. There were records of him making small payments for guns to be forged during 1473-4, but in the main he relied on his father's artillery, and begged additions from Louis XI of France or Archduke Sigismund of Austria until, in the face of a likely and major attack by the English, he spent the relatively modest sum of £214 4s. for 'the makin of serpentynis and gunnys.'[32]

In spite of this, James III showed himself a modest military reformer: going further than his father and grandfather in recognising the need for a Scottish navy and in funding the *Yellow Carvel*, an armed merchantman, together with spending on other ships, probably for short-term hire.[33] Quite apart from Scotland's greater involvement with Europe there were other good reasons for her forces to include some naval craft. Ship-borne transport was clearly required, for instance, for James III's ambitious scheme of invading Brittany in 1472, while without some form of protection Scottish trade to the Baltic continued to be vulnerable to privateers, whether or not they were sponsored by other nations. When challenges to the crown from the Western Isles required the king's presence in 1476 he proceeded there by way of the Forth estuary, apparently in the *Yellow Carvel*.

Above all, James III came to realise some counter was needed to England's aggression at sea. An early grievance occurred in 1473 when Bishop Kennedy's famous barge, the *Salvator*, was seized near Bamburgh by an Englishman, James Ker, for which England agreed to pay compensation. Far more serious was Edward IV's decision in 1481, during England's short war with Scotland, to grant authority to Lord Howard and Sir Thomas Fulford 'to keep the western seas' and with it the power to take Scottish ships. With this assurance Howard sailed unopposed into the Firth of Forth, and following his burning of Blackness, took as prizes eight ships from Leith, Kinghorn and Pittenweem.

James III's performance as king of Scotland has earned almost universal condemnation, not only for his meanness but also for his exaggerated insistence on the regard due to him as king. In this respect his biographer, Norman MacDougall, judged him as 'an aloof, overbearing and vindictive ruler whose dangerously exalted concept of Scottish kingship confounded his friends and eventually proved a godsend to his enemies.'[34]

In his relations with other countries James III not only embarked on the unpopular cause of seeking friendship with England, however sound this might have proved in the long term, but dealt with Europe as if he was its premier monarch, and within Scotland he trusted no one, rewarded no one and mounted frequent and unjustifiable attacks on the Scottish nobility as a whole. Above all, he was 'acutely mistrustful of his kin'. In 1479 he had his brother Albany arrested and charged with breaking the truce with England, but Albany escaped from Edinburgh Castle by roping his way down one of its precipitous rock faces and fled to France. James' youngest brother, Mar, was also arrested and died in suspicious circumstances, probably in a bath while being bled. Bishop Lesley described the event succinctly enough. 'They cuttit ane of his vanes and causit him bleid to dead.'[35]

James sought help from England to capture Albany but Edward IV who, in the face of Scottish border raids and the loss of Berwick, no longer valued their truce so highly, saw Albany as a means of unsettling the Scottish king. He even agreed to sponsor Albany as an alternative king of Scotland and promised his daughter to him in marriage, providing he broke with France and surrendered Berwick. This reversion to England's earlier policy of Scottish king-making was further demonstrated when Edward IV sent a powerful English army northwards under the command of his brother, the Duke of Gloucester (the future Richard III), an army larger than any sent to Scotland during the previous eighty years. It was well equipped, all its members were paid for a month from mid-July to mid-August, and it contained a chosen element whose wages were guaranteed for a longer period so that they could complete the anticipated siege of Berwick Castle.[36] In response, James led out the Scottish host, complete with its artillery train, and it moved south from Edinburgh. Like his predecessors James had already proved the potency of his artillery in a successful siege of Albany's castle, but it was not to be used against the English. The Scottish nobility were appalled at the likely military outcome: they seized James and the army was disbanded, leaving Gloucester to march upon a defenceless Edinburgh.

After lengthy negotiations James was restored to power although, in 1484 when Gloucester became Richard III of England and the two countries agreed a three-year truce, Berwick remained in English hands. The next year civil war returned to England when Richard III was defeated and killed by forces led by Henry Tudor (later Henry VII) on Bosworth Field. Henry VII's accession promised better relations between the two countries but it came too late for James III who, by his avarice and double-dealing, had even alienated the Duke of Argyll, his faithful supporter and brought against him the Homes, that most powerful border family, together with their allies, the Hepburns. More serious still, the king's attempts to overthrow the Homes sparked off a rebellion by his eldest son, the Duke of Rothesay, whom he had kept a virtual prisoner.

The royal forces clashed with the rebels led by the prince on 11 June 1488 at the Sauchieburn, close to Bannockburn. Neither side used artillery and in spite of their larger numbers the royalists, some of whose loyalty was questionable, were pushed back. James III was wearing the sword used by Robert Bruce at Bannockburn, but not even this talisman could improve his showing as a commander; he left the field in the battle's early stages and was unhorsed while leaping the Bannock burn. He was carried unconscious into Beaton's Mill close by, where, on recovering his senses, he called for a priest; a stranger purporting to be one entered – and stabbed him four or five times to the heart. Thus ended James III's inglorious kingship at the age of thirty-six, to be succeeded by his very different and able heir.

It was as well James III had sought peaceful relations with England, given his habit of provoking trouble within his own country and because of his limited military acumen. For both countries a more stable period was now in prospect: the strong Tudor, Henry VII, had already held the English throne for three years and, with the accession of James IV, who would prove himself the most effective Scottish king since Robert Bruce and the last to enjoy support from the whole of Scotland, both countries possessed proud and determined monarchs.

In England, Henry VII had by now shown the courage and diplomatic skills that enabled him to found a dynasty which was to last for over 100 years and which, in his son Henry VIII and granddaughter Elizabeth I, would become 'the quintessence of Englishry and the focus of swelling national pride'.[37]

With increased confidence on both sides it was possible the old conflict between England and Scotland would flare up again. With greater resources and advancing technology the monarchs in both countries could delight in new weapon systems that appeared to offer clear-cut military successes and be tempted to see war more in terms of martial contests or as gauges of personal and national virility than uniformly in support of vital national interests. Such specialisation appeared to favour the wealthier adversary and bring fresh dangers for the defenders of a relatively poor but immensely proud country like Scotland.

But unlike the period of the Wars of Independence, when

Scottish moves across the border were mounted to counter earlier English aggression, and when a great stand-up battle, like Bannockburn, was needed to consolidate the successes of Robert Bruce's scorched-earth tactics, Scotland faced no similar threats. In such circumstances there seemed a greater likelihood that attempts to bring the two countries together peacefully, which had in earlier times seemed possible but had proved untimely, might be repeated with a greater chance of success.

Whether England and Scotland opted for continuing peace or reverted to war, which in the climate of the time promised a return to large-scale encounters, would, as in the past four hundred years, depend primarily on the personalities and ambitions of their respective kings.

≈

CHAPTER TWO

PROUD MONARCHS

Burning pride and high disdain
Sir Walter Scott, *The Lay of the Last Minstrel*

A S A CHILD, the Lancastrian Henry Tudor, with apparently little chance of gaining the English throne, was brought up in relative obscurity in Wales. He was then exiled for fifteen years in dangerous and straitened circumstances in Brittany and France. After his victory at Bosworth, with Henry's opponent, Richard III, lying dead on the battlefield, a frantic search was made for the crown, the ultimate symbol of royal authority. The battered golden circlet was eventually discovered under a hawthorn bush from where it was retrieved and, to the acclamation of his soldiers, placed on Henry's head. In fact, Henry VII's title to the crown was no better than other claimants from the opposing royal line of York, but he reinforced his position by marrying Elizabeth of York, thus ending the bitter rivalry which precipitated the Wars of the Roses: eight months later she bore him a son. Henry further strengthened his position by calling a parliament which reversed its attainder against him, acknowledged his legal right to the throne and granted him a subsidy.

Soon after his accession Henry took good care to reward his leading supporters, especially Bishop John Morton, who was to become his chancellor, and Bishop Richard Fox, the keeper of the Privy Seal; most of them returned his confidence by staying in their offices all their working lives. Notwithstanding, Henry ruled over a kingdom that remained unsettled and during his first twelve years he was forced to face a succession of rebellions before he was able to establish a clear ascendancy and show other nations that his Tudor dynasty was firmly based.

During the initial two years of his reign serious challenges were mounted by Lambert Simnel and Perkin Warbeck, both pretenders to his throne. In 1497 there was an uprising in the west country, when the Cornish and Devonshire men marched on London but were conclusively defeated. In such circumstances it is not surprising that Henry VII became known for his caution and watchfulness.

At the beginning of his reign peace with England's near neighbours was of prime importance to him, and throughout it he retained his core belief that he had much to lose, and probably little to gain, by going to war. Conflicts were bound to involve major risks by encouraging dangerous internal factions that could interrupt his legislative reforms and reverse his avowed policy of steadily accumulating his own and his country's wealth. He had demonstrated his personal bravery at Bosworth and had no desire to pursue vain glory, although he was determined to establish his authority over his nobles. In his more mature years his undoubted acquisitiveness bordered on avarice and led to a series of arbitrary and unjust acts against wealthy individuals. Yet he remained the most cautious of kings, for he considered that England's external status should accurately reflect its power-base, independent of diplomatic coups and unburdened by dreams of expansion such as those held by earlier Plantagenet monarchs.

But as Pope Sixtus V observed, 'England was only half an island' – there was always Scotland to consider.[1] Henry VII was fortunate in that his pugnacious neighbour was ruled, in the first instance, by a monarch who uncharacteristically pursued a peaceful policy with him. After three years, when James III was replaced by his son, it seemed likely that more traditional attitudes towards England would be resumed but a due interval could reasonably be expected before the fifteen-year-old king exerted his full authority. In fact, seven years passed before James IV's nominee, William Elphinstone, Bishop of Aberdeen, became the Privy Seal and the king began to rule personally over his country. By then the Scottish establishment could not doubt the depth of Henry VII's commitment to peace between the two countries.

James IV of Scotland was in every way more flamboyant and energetic with an impressive range of interests. The then Spanish ambassador, Don Pedro de Ayala, wrote glowingly of him, although of course it was in his interests to do so. It is worth noting, too, that J.D. Mackie, one of Scotland's prominent historians, thinks much less well of him than did Ayala. James IV was addicted to sport, as was his future rival Henry VIII of England, and he was a notable horseman, but he spent more of his time on affairs of state than Henry VIII, who preferred to find ministers to do this for him. James was no great reader – George Buchanan ungraciously remarked that he had 'a keen but uncultivated intelligence'[2] – but he was a competent linguist and also very devout, always toying with the idea of a crusade. In one respect he never faltered, namely in his extreme pride in being king of Scotland: not only was he intensely proud of his people but, very revealingly, they were as proud of him. He was not parsimonious; so interested was he in hawking that he once paid the amazing sum of £180 for a single bird[3] and above all he could be lavish when it enhanced his power and promoted his state interests. Nothing could have exceeded the grandeur of his reception for his future English bride when, despite his slender revenues, he spent £6125 4s. 6d. on his wedding.[4]

Yet James probably had as many mistresses as Charles II. One was Margaret Drummond, who with her two sisters was poisoned by the king's advisers and buried with them under great blue stones in Dunblane cathedral. But like Charles II they were subordinated to his statecraft; not so subject was his passion for the glamour and the show of war.

No previous king made more sumptuous provisions for tournaments, the traditional training grounds for conflict, than James IV. However, his delight at appearing in tournaments as the 'wild knycht' (about whose identity scarcely anyone would be deceived) could not compare with the pleasures of watching his cannon pounding castles 'in anger', and in seeing his flagship the *Great Michael* grow from the keel upwards. His great guns and great ship fascinated him even more than war itself and though personally brave, as he showed at Flodden, he was not a born warrior in the mould of Robert Bruce. It was the panoply and the perumbria of war that interested him as much as the actual fighting.

No one could doubt James' enthusiasm for military matters, but it is in their assessment of his martial skills that James' commentators appear most at variance. In probably the most widely known comment on him, made, in reference to his 1496 campaign, Ayala said of James, 'He is courageous even more than a king should be ... I have seen him undertake most dangerous things in the last wars ... He is not a good captain because he begins to fight before he has given his orders.'[5] More sweeping than this criticism of a young man who so obviously believed his position required him to court danger, was Professor Mackie's scorching assessment of James when he was approaching forty. Mackie says that he was no wary, disillusioned statesman, but a 'moonstruck romantic whose eyes were ever at the ends of the earth'.[6] His later biographer, Norman MacDougall, thought differently and fully acknowledged James' instinctive grasp of the essentials of Scottish kingship, the need both to lead by example and simultaneously preserve an internal balance throughout his kingdom. In commenting on James' foreign policy, however, MacDougall is not only similarly approving of the Scottish king's actions but crushingly dismissive of Henry VIII. To MacDougall, James IV was subtle-minded enough to see himself as 'a popular king joining his French ally in an effort to check the absurd European pretensions of England's bellicose and immature ruler, seeking at the same time to provide plunder for the host and a substantial strategic gain for himself.'

No one denies that James prepared for war over many years and in the final part of his reign lavished far more on it than any other item of royal expenditure, but there were perfectly sound reasons for this, quite apart from the king's fascination with military affairs. James needed military success; he needed to obtain oaths of allegiance from chiefs in the Western Isles to overcome any dissident nobles within Scotland. And, like Europe's other contemporary sovereigns, he was expected not only to possess the means of defending his country but, if necessary, to take offensive measures in the furtherance of its cause, such as recovering those castles still in English hands.

In all countries, but particularly in the case of a relatively poor country such as Scotland, there would always be limits to such military expenditure. Consequently James continued to rely for the most part on the country's traditional host of able-bodied men between sixteen and sixty, that in times of national crisis could be embodied for a maximum of forty days so that, as with the first two Jameses, most of James IV's expenditure – at least where his land forces were concerned – was on the Scottish artillery train.

This arm had already caught his imagination when, as a king of sixteen and still a long way from gaining control over his councillors, a rebellion occurred in the north-east of Scotland on behalf of the late king, his father. It was then that he first watched the great cannons, including Mons Meg and 'the gun subsequently called Duchal' that were dragged with such difficulty from Edinburgh, pounding the castle of Duchal. A little later, Dumbarton Castle presented a far more formidable target, holding out for seven months until the big guns, including 'Duchal', floated across the Clyde on three boats, were brought up to pulverise it. The royal cannons were also brought into action at the siege of Tantallon Castle in 1491.

When he was twenty-two and by that point unquestionable master of Scotland, he offered support to Perkin Warbeck, pretender to the English throne, which was not only designed to unsettle Henry VII but also to provide the opportunity for retaking Berwick. By the time Warbeck arrived in Scotland he was largely discredited, having been rejected in Europe and having already taken part in two unsuccessful landings, one on English soil at Deal in Kent, the other at Waterford in Ireland. However, during November 1495 James welcomed him, together with his motley group of followers, and dubbed him Prince Richard of England. At the same time James gave orders for military 'wappenshaws' – musters to test the country's military readiness – to be held across Scotland.[7] Such assemblies served as a threat to England but they were also expected to help James calculate what actual assistance he might give to Warbeck. Another measure of James' support for the pretender came with his approval of a marriage between Warbeck and Lady Catherine Gordon, daughter of George, second Earl of Huntly, no more than a distant cousin of the king but reputedly the most beautiful woman in Scotland.

Such initiatives brought a positive response from Henry VII. He ordered his advisers to commence negotiations with a view to a marriage between his daughter, Margaret, and the Scottish king, for he appreciated how much it was in his interest that permanent friendly relations should be established between the two countries.[8] As Margaret was only six, the proposed marriage would not be able to take place for some years and consequently James felt little pressure to scale down warlike preparations, raising a levy on the whole country for this purpose.[9] This course of action shows James closer to MacDougall's Machiavellian concept of him than Mackie's more impulsive picture, particularly as he also took pains to extract undertakings from Warbeck, in the slim hope that the contender might succeed in attracting military support from the disaffected English northern counties; were this to happen Warbeck agreed to pay a grant of more than 50,000 marks, and hand over the border fortress of Berwick.

James assembled a reasonably sized army, including his prized artillery, whose entourage of craftsmen and labourers were hired for just fourteen days at the cost of £270 10s.[10] In a lightning twelve-day campaign James' army crossed the Tweed at Coldstream and devastated part of Northumberland, while Warbeck himself, finding no support there and reputedly shocked by the Scots' vigorous sacking and looting, crossed back into Scotland after only a single day's campaigning. Anticipating the later Flodden campaign the Scottish artillery destroyed the five towers of Twizel, Tillmouth, Duddo, Branxton and Howtel in the Tweed and Till valleys and were engaged in besieging Heton Castle when reports were received of an English army moving up from Newcastle. At this, James broke off hostilities and withdrew across the border. According to the Spaniard, Ayala, the king had exposed himself to quite unnecessary dangers, yet he came off unscathed and he could feel he had not only demonstrated his martial abilities but also given his artillery campaigning practice before making a prudent withdrawal in the face of serious danger.

James might reasonably have believed he could risk such limited aggression against Henry VII but Henry was very angry, particularly at James' continued support for the pretender, and his response surpassed all Scottish expectations. Henry proclaimed the seven-year truce between both countries broken, gave his subjects permission to make war on the Scots by land or sea (which in practical terms meant against Scottish merchant ships) and, at a meeting of his Great Council, requested a staggering grant of £120,000 sterling (more than twenty times the Scottish king's normal revenue) with the avowed purpose of equipping 'an enormous army and fleet to invade Scotland'.[11] Undaunted, James continued to plan offensive measures of his own, including the southwards movement of his artillery and, on 12 February 1497, he allowed the Homes to make a sizeable raid across the border. In spite of James' continuing aggression, the movement of large English armies northwards was to augur ill for the Scots in any renewed border warfare, but in the event a combination of luck and Henry's excessive reaction turned things in the Scots' favour. The English king's well deserved reputation for greed, together with his calls for heavy taxation, caused this latest demand to spark off a revolt in the west country, bringing thousands of men from Cornwall and Devon led by a blacksmith, Michael Joseph, in a march on London. Although Henry saw them off in battle at Blackheath, near Guildford, the unrest continued and, realising the time was not opportune to send his soldiers northwards, he despatched Richard Fox, Bishop of Durham, to offer James peace if he would surrender Warbeck. James complied – although he kept Warbeck out of Henry's hands by sending him to Ireland, not England.

James, however, aware of the continuing unrest in England, immediately began to draw up plans for another border offensive, which this time would include the use of his heavy guns. But such plans required further expenditure and the Scottish king's dire shortage of funds to pay for both the artillery and its ancillary personnel became clear when, in addition to a general levy in support of his campaign, prominent nobles were prevailed upon to make special contributions: the sums obtained included £236 17s. from the king's brother, who had recently been made archbishop of St Andrews, and £100 from the Abbot of Arbroath.[12] In reality, because of the temporary nature of Henry's problems and the size of English resources in the border regions or within easy march of them, Scotland's chances of major military success appeared small. The country was simply too poor for such ambitious ventures.

On 20 July 1497, soldiers from the Scottish host south of the Forth duly mustered for another offensive against Norham Castle on the English bank of the Tweed six miles west of Berwick; if captured it could conceivably be exchanged for Berwick itself. The massive Scottish artillery train brought down from Edinburgh blasted Norham from the Tweed's northern (Scottish) bank, while at the same time Scottish foot soldiers crossed the river to ravage the surrounding English countryside. However, James had only engaged the craftsmen and labourers needed to service his artillery for a week, a period subsequently doubled to a fortnight. Even then, in spite of James' levy and the financial help provided by individuals, the king was forced to melt down part of his own massive gold chain of office to raise a further £571 towards the expense. When the castle successfully held out and an English relief force approached under the Earl of Surrey, James was forced to break off the siege and return to Edinburgh. Having achieved its objective Surrey's army also soon withdrew and on 5 September 1497 Henry VII sent his commissioners northwards to treat for peace.

That such English peace initiatives should follow James' moves across the border and his removal of considerable plunder to Scotland are revealing. Henry knew James did not constitute a grievous military threat since he did not possess the military resources necessary to penetrate far into the English Marcher counties. Besides, the attention of the English king was set on a far greater prize than exacting petty revenge: the ultimate result, and triumph, of Henry's diplomacy was the agreement for a marriage between James and Margaret, due to take place during August 1503 when Margaret would be almost fourteen years of age. This would seal a proposed treaty of perpetual peace between both countries running from 1502 onwards, and in the event of any further disputes between them Ferdinand and Isabella of Spain were appointed as arbiters.[13] But although such a treaty brought the prospect of union between England and Scotland closer it also brought risks for Henry, since the Tudor succession seemed less secure than that of the Stewarts, and some of his advisers questioned what would happen if a Scottish king were to rule both kingdoms. Henry's confident and prescient answer was that Scotland would, in that case, be an accession to England, not England to Scotland, 'for that the greater would draw the less'.[14]

The greatest danger for Scotland from the king's warlike posturing and Henry's pacific reaction was that as a lover of war James might become deluded regarding his military strength. James had certainly done all he could to improve his country's advanced weaponry, as he not only built up his armoury of cannon but spent large sums in his effort to make

Scotland a sea power, but this could easily mislead a king who had often shown himself to be more sanguine than sensible.

James' fascination with ships began even earlier than his appreciation of heavy artillery. At the beginning of August 1488 the fifteen-year-old monarch was permitted to visit Leith and go on board the Danish ships that had probably brought his great-uncle Gerhard of Oldenburg to Scotland. From that time on James determined to have his own ships and by August 1506 he was able to tell the French king, Louis XII, that his long-standing plan to build a Scottish fleet to defend his country was near fruition.[15] Although this was something of an exaggeration, James' expenditure on his navy, not only on building or buying ships but also on their crew and maintenance, was indeed very large, inordinately so for a country with Scotland's relatively meagre resources. Of course, his order that boats of twenty tons burden or more be constructed in all Scotland's seaport towns also promised economic advantages by helping to develop Scottish fisheries.[16] Such materialistic reasoning, though, was more characteristic of Henry VII than the Stewart who, above anything else, wanted his own navy to do with as he pleased.

If a fleet was indeed needed to defend Scotland the most likely threat could only come from England, since any danger from Norway had disappeared with the Scottish victory at Largs in 1263 and the subsequent annexation of Orkney and Shetland by James III. The English had already demonstrated the value of naval power when they resupplied and reinforced their armies during major invasions of Scotland by the three Edwards, but that was two hundred years before, when England had aimed to subjugate Scotland. This was never Henry VII's policy, in spite of his furious reactions to James' sponsoring of Perkin Warbeck. In the eyes of the Scottish king, however, things would never appear so clear-cut, although he was aware how, in the summer of 1482, amid the convulsions of his father's reign, the large English army under the joint command of Gloucester and James III's brother, Albany, had invaded south-eastern Scotland with the benefit of naval support. Such dual service co-operation had also helped to bring about the fall of Berwick in 1482, while in the previous year English ships had made their way through the Forth to Edinburgh's port of Leith and seized the Scottish ships berthed there. In fact this marked the high point in English fifteenth-century sea power at the time when Thomas Rogers, an ex sea-captain and champion of naval forces, held the post of clerk of the king's ships and had fifteen ships under his control.[17]

At Henry VII's accession, the English navy was reduced to five ships and it remained at this low level until the end of his reign, although this total included modern vessels such as the *Regent* and the *Sovereign* that were more potent than their predecessors, and the king also issued orders for the first dry dock to be built at Portsmouth. However, this relatively small nucleus was capable of being expanded by chartering merchant ships and their crews, who were to be paid at normal naval rates when on regular service. The cost of hiring such ships was set at a shilling a ton per month and they could subsequently be armed with guns and bows and arrows from the royal store at Greenwich. Although Henry's commercial instincts led him to build up the English merchant navy, it remained a flexible instrument that was further strengthened when Henry offered a bounty to encourage the building or purchase of ships large enough to fight.[18]

To make his service viable Henry passed acts requiring imported goods to be carried in English, Irish or Welsh ships, a move almost certain to bring friction with Scotland since, even at times of truce, there were instances when armed ships, with or without Henry's knowledge, attacked merchant ships entering Scottish waters from abroad. Pitscottie describes how during the summer of 1489, five such English ships attacked and plundered Scottish merchantmen in the Firth of Forth until the famous Scottish captain Sir Andrew Wood, soon to become a hero in James' eyes, attacked with his two armed ships, the *Yellow Carvel* and the *Flower*, compelling the English to surrender and carrying them back in triumph to Leith.[19]

James' first use of his navy was against the rebellious lords of the Western Isles. In 1494 he sailed there to receive their allegiance but on his return to Edinburgh they rose against him once more. An urgent repair and rebuilding programme was carried out at Dumbarton in the winter of 1494–5, and during the following spring the king moved by sea to Mingay Castle on the Sound of Mull, there to receive again the submission of the western chiefs.[20]

By the turn of the century, James IV had very little to fear, either from the chiefs in the west who were now contributing to the royal revenue, or from offensive moves by England. However, James was not satisfied simply protecting Scottish merchant shipping; he sought to safeguard his country from possible attacks in the future when English ships could either support their land armies or carry troops to attack Scottish east coast towns. This policy was confirmed when he sited a fort by Queen's Ferry where the Forth narrowed, and went on to develop shipyards, one at a 'New Havin', about a mile to the west of Leith, and another at the Pool of Airth, eight miles south-east of Stirling.

The pattern of James IV's military expenditure demonstrated his deepening commitment to his fleet. For the first ten years of his reign the accumulated total spent on it was £1482 12s. 10d., putting the annual costs at only about £140 (admittedly loaded by a separate figure of £500 spent on a new barge for sailing to the Western Isles). During 1501–4 this had risen almost fourfold to £600 a year and during 1507–8 he spent £7279. By 1511–13, with a new king on the English throne, annual spending on the fleet had grown to £8710. 10s.[21] Although these costs were apparently understated, they show that over a twenty-five-year period when royal income only trebled, the king's expenditure on his navy increased more than sixtyfold, with the greatest rise in the years shortly before 1513.

In hindsight it can be seen that such vast expenditure on his land cannon and navy did not enhance Scotland's security in any way proportionate to the cost and that James might well have taken wiser courses of action. He might, for instance, have built up funds to pay soldiers or hire mercenaries for specific land campaigns or, alternatively, have opted for the cheaper naval option of hiring ships and manning them with his own trusted captains. But he was not naturally prudent and such ships would not be truly his, nor would they satisfy his image of regal strength and his love of display. In the event, just four ships came to be wholly owned by the king, the *Margaret*, the *James*, the *Treasurer* and the *Michael*. Of these, the *Michael* (or *Great Michael* as people knew her) was the largest, taking some five years to build: Pitscottie, writing in the 1570s, said the *Michael* was so large it 'waisit all the wodis in Fyfe except Falkland wode by [besides] all the Pymmer that was gotten out of Noraway.' In fact, this 1000-ton monster needed additional timber from Denmark and France and Pitscottie put its cost at an incredible £30,000 Scots. Of equal delight to the king were her guns, twelve large weapons on each side and three enormous basilisks, one forward and two aft. When it took to the water the *Michael* was the most powerful ship afloat until, a year later, Henry VIII launched his *Henri Grâce à Dieu* – the Great Harry – of 1400 tons carrying similar armament. Characteristically, James frequently visited his shipyards and gave himself the rank of admiral-in-chief, together with the insignia of admiral's whistle and gold chain. No Scottish king had a closer association with his sailors.

James' military expenditure was, of course, by no means the only cause of worsening relations with England. The replacement in 1509 of a cautious, acquisitive, tubercular-ridden king of fifty-two who for half his reign faced challenges to his throne, with a highly popular young man of seventeen, in full physical vigour, possessing an unchallengeable right to the throne and a treasure chest bulging with one and a quarter million pounds, was always going to bring significant changes

[53]

in policy. In England as a whole there was rejoicing when the acquisitive Henry VII was replaced by a comely young king capable of a graciousness and charm unequalled by his father. By the standards of his day Henry VIII was extraordinarily handsome and powerful; he was also strong, well above average height, and could apparently draw a longbow further and fire it with greater accuracy than any of his contemporaries. His biographer Scarisbrick memorably described the young Henry as a 'rumbustious, noisy, unbottomed, prodigal man, exulting in his magnificent physique, boisterous animal exercise, orgies of gambling and eating, lavish clothes.'[22] Even more than James IV, Henry loved adornment: his fingers were covered in jewelled rings and according to the Venetian ambassador he wore a gold collar round his neck from which hung a diamond as big as a walnut. Like Henry, James too was splendidly apparelled, wearing a soft bonnet with a huge, fiery red ruby fixed on it. But whereas Henry VIII, until he later developed his gross paunch, gave the impression of a burly and athletic king, James IV, while remarkably fit and energetic and moderate in his eating and drinking, appeared more of a dreamer and a poet than a resolute king.

There was, however, far more to Henry than animal spirits. Knowledgeable in Latin and French, together with some Italian and Spanish, he was probably a better linguist than James, and with Henry's education for the church, his biblical and theological knowledge was wide-reaching. He was interested in mathematics and astronomy but above all such pursuits came a love for music: he played a range of instruments and composed many songs and instrumental pieces, even two five-part masses. With such wide accomplishments Henry could reasonably refer to himself as a very perfect valorous knight. And, as he indulged himself in searching for pleasure he began dispensing favours with his father's treasure – £335 to Jacques Maryn, a jeweller of Paris, £566 for a thousand pearls and other jewels and £40 to a friar who gave the king an instrument.[23] James IV was not alone in his profligacy but Henry had, of course, far more money at his disposal.

Another biographer, professor Pollard concluded that Henry's intellect, will and character did not mature until many years after he came to the throne. At the age of 18, however, his pride was no less than his ignorance of affairs. Pausing for once to look more closely at a letter he had just signed to the King of France he discovered to his disgust that he had sued for peace. He shouted out, 'I ask for peace of the King of France who dare not look me in the face, still less make war on me?'[24] It was the tone of a young man whose energy and idealism would turn for full release on the battlefield and although, initially, he did not stray far from his father's policies, before his first twelve months on the throne were over he had ordered his subjects to furnish themselves with weapons of war for which the long peace had left them unprepared.

Not content with attending to the readiness of his levies he also determined to increase his country's naval strength. Within the first year of his reign he had authorised the building of the *Mary Rose*, weighing 600 tons, and the *Peter Pomegranate* of 450 tons. Soon afterwards he gave orders for the construction of the *Great Henry Imperial* or *Henry Grâce à Dieu* (the Great Harry), the largest and most powerful ship on earth, dwarfing James IV's *Great Michael* which had consumed so much of the Scottish king's available capital and time. The *Great Harry* took more than four years to build and was not officially blessed until its launching in 1514. In the meantime Henry continued to buy other ships and also took care to retain his father's power of authority for hiring merchantmen when needed.[25] To Henry, like James, ships were not merely items in his war armoury, but things of genuine interest and, not unjustly, he has been called the 'father of the English Navy'. It was under Henry's control that tiers of gun ports were set into the waists of boats, thus introducing into naval warfare the possibility of broadsides.

Henry VIII also enlarged the dry dock at Portsmouth

set up by his father, as well as building Woolwich dock-
yard in 1514, and Deptford somewhat later. He licensed the
incorporation of Trinity House, which was charged with the
advancement of navigation, pilotage and commerce, and set
up the body which would eventually become the Navy Board.
Like his Scottish counterpart, he had a fascination for guns
and enjoyed seeing his ships' heavy guns fired again and
again. He also delighted in the roar and discharge of his land
cannon, including a dozen large cannon made for him by the
Flemish gunsmith Poppenruyter in 1513, inevitably dubbed
'the Twelve Apostles'.

At this time Henry could be seen as an 'archtype of resplend-
ent Renaissance monarchy',[26] a king who, like James, watched
over and strengthened his country's sinews of war. Contrary
to his father, he came to adopt an interventionist policy which
was aided from 1512 onwards by his outstanding minister,
Thomas Wolsey, and showed himself fully prepared to revive
traditional English prejudices in his relationship with France
and Scotland. Any pinpricks inflicted by the northern kingdom
were now liable to be returned with interest.

In Henry VIII, James IV faced a warlike king, arrogant,
ambitious, ruthless and unpredictable. For long periods both
England and Scotland had been weakened by inter-baronial
rivalry, but now two strong rulers, with little love for each
other, had the ability to keep their supporting nobles firmly
under control and the means to mobilise national armies of
unequalled strength. It was time for the levies to check their
weapons.

CHAPTER THREE

————————————— ≈ —————————————

SLIDE TOWARDS WAR

No man has ever served at the same time his passions
and his best interests

Sallust, *The War with Cataline*

W ITHIN FOUR AND a half years of Henry VIII coming to
the English throne the political climate between Scotland and England changed radically. In 1509 both countries
were bound by the treaty of perpetual peace concluded seven
years earlier by Henry VII and James IV, with its key obligation
that 'If any other prince should wage war against one of the
contracting parties the other, upon demand, shall aid him . . .'[1]
While the treaty had been sealed by the marriage of Henry
VII's daughter Margaret – Henry VIII's sister – to the Scottish
king, its framers were also acute enough to recognise the
likelihood of future strains arising between both countries,
and wise enough to emphasise that such occurrences, whether
on the border or on the high seas, were deemed not to
constitute a breach of the main treaty. But in spite of such
far-sighted precautions, by 1513 Scotland and England were
at war. This was in considerable part due to the extent
of the personal antipathy that developed between James IV
and Henry VIII, although the root causes came from events
elsewhere in Europe.

In the later Middle Ages the Europe of feudal states under
Emperor and Pope was evolving into a collection of separate
nation states led by powerful autocratic, if generally popular,
rulers intent on pursuing their own dynastic, national and
religious interests. The predominant protagonist was undoubtedly France, where large, fertile territories and an affluent
bourgeoisie gave its crown the capital to raise a professional

army, including mercenaries, and to develop into an efficient bureaucratic state. Its king had been able to assimilate parts of Burgundy, Provence and Brittany before, in 1494, he sent his soldiers to pour over the Alps onto the wealthy plains of Italy. The fallout from such aggression combined to move Scotland and England into rival camps.

The other notable and powerful European states at the time were Spain, the Hapsburg dominions and, latterly, England. In Spain, Ferdinand of Aragon had married Isabella of Castile and together they succeeded in driving the Moors from Granada and conquering the whole of the Iberian peninsula. With its own interests in Italy, Spain could not be expected to remain passive as France invaded that country. Furthemore, it had developed a powerful connection with England when Ferdinand's daughter, Catherine, had married Henry VII's eldest son, Arthur and, following Arthur's death, married his brother, who became Henry VIII. After Catherine became Queen of England, Ferdinand, the wiliest of monarchs, intended to further his own designs by persuading Henry to attack France and began to work through his daughter to this end.

The French invasion of Italy was also of acute interest to Maximilian I, the Holy Roman Emperor, who, by marrying Mary, daughter of Charles the Bold, Duke of Burgundy, had joined the Netherlands to Hapsburg Austria, thereby extending his interests to the very borders of his rival, France.

In the case of England, the thrifty and unwarlike Henry VII had enabled his country to regain its once powerful European position by ending the internal divisions endemic during the prolonged Wars of the Roses and by carefully building up his coffers. Henry VII's policy was to keep England clear of European quarrels, but Henry VIII's more aggressive nature would virtually guarantee England's renewed involvement in Europe against French expansion. This would have serious new implications for England's relations with Scotland, the natural ally of France.[2] In Scotland from 1488 onwards James

IV's increasingly strong government succeeded in further unifying his nation and greatly increasing the royal revenue. And Scotland, apart from seeing France as its traditional ally, was both proud and flattered to be asked to join in wider European councils, particularly during 1510 when James IV attempted to reconcile Pope Julius II with the French king. James' increased interest in Europe added to the unlikelihood that he would remain passive while England attacked France.

France's invasion of Italy was made easier because the latter continued to lack a central authority: in the north separate states were left to negotiate their own internal alliances; in the centre the Papacy, which had already lost a degree of its religious authority, was concerned with creating a temporal Italian kingdom of its own; while further south the kingdoms of Naples and Sicily pursued their independent course. Even so, it was in Renaissance Italy where the modern state emerged, the state whose whole being was expressed in power and which looked to its prince to safeguard and extend it by all means, however immoral. But whereas much could be learned by other European states about the nature of the modern state from Machiavelli's books, *The Prince* and *The Discourses*, based on the behaviour of Machiavelli's Medici ruler, or for that matter from his distillation of military history in *The Art of War*,[3] Italian developments were on a relatively small scale. The modern state was born in the larger countries outside Italy, springing from the roots of the bastard feudalism of the Middle Ages but nurtured by their increasingly strong military establishments. Their new artillery could, for instance, break down the strongest fortress walls. Although wars had never been cheap, such developments tended to make them increasingly expensive. Nevertheless, the growing wealth of their middle classes still gave the larger powers of Europe the wherewithal to fight. Support from the Fuggers, a great banking family, was, for instance, invaluable in helping the Emperor Charles V to fight his wars.

As a result, the premier European powers – France, Spain,

the Empire of the Hapsburgs and England – familiar as they were with the writings of Machiavelli, plunged with enthusiasm into the maelstrom of this early modern period. War at this time was endemic and everything appeared to be in play. The frontiers of states were not yet clearly defined and, since territorial possession was still seen as the most reliable indication of a state's power, Europe's rulers sought to extend their boundaries. The Compte de Seyssel, for instance, stressed in his book *La Monarchie de France*, published in 1515, the importance of making new conquests by sewing dissension among one's neighbours.

The modern state emerged in Europe amid a welter of conflict and in conditions which made the continuation of Henry VII's policy of disengagement well nigh impossible. In any event, from the time of his succession Henry VIII began to embark on a number of adventurous and erratic initiatives. After announcing he would soon attack France[4] he publicly insulted the French ambassador before bothering to consult his father-in-law and ally, Ferdinand of Aragon, who considered such an attack premature.[5] Then, in 1510, he made a treaty with France and two months later another with Spain which virtually annulled his treaty with France. In 1511 he was at it again, joining the Holy League which the Pope was assembling against France and receiving from the Pope as a traditional mark of favour, a golden rose, together with a hundred parmesan cheeses and barrels of wine.

During the same year Henry despatched two expeditions, each of about 1500 men, in support of France's enemies. The first, which included a good proportion of bowmen, were under the command of Sir Edward Poynings to help the Hapsburg queen Margaret of the Netherlands against a rebellion raised by the French Duke of Gelders, a cousin of the Stewarts. This prompted James IV to warn Henry that if he joined with the Emperor in attacking Gelders he would be regarded as an enemy. Characteristically, Henry ignored the warning and went ahead. The second of Henry's sorties which sailed from Plymouth under Lord Darcy to join in Ferdinand's attack upon the Moors, arrived in Cadiz to find itself unwanted and, following riotous behaviour by its soldiers, it returned home after a fortnight.

Professor Scarisbrick, for one, was in no doubt whatever about Henry's grave lack of responsibility over such actions, emphasising that, as well as quickly dissipating his inherited treasure, he did nothing to serve England's national interests: 'his new stance was largely due to personal self-indulgence . . . his forward continental policy was not in pursuit of any vital ends such as Lebensraum, national frontiers or political advantage. On the contrary it was occasionally clearly opposed to at least the last mentioned.'[6]

Rash as some of their actions undoubtedly were, neither Henry VIII nor James IV were prepared to let their ministers govern for them. Although James' veteran adviser Bishop William Elphinstone long stood high in his regard, by 1513 James had rejected his advice against making war with England. And Wolsey's influence on Henry rested solely on his adroitness in enabling Henry to do what he wanted. Henry and James were both acting in the way of other European rulers in their prepared-ness to go to war if they reckoned it would benefit themselves as much as their countries. Such attitudes provoked the renowned Humanist treatises against war, namely Erasmus' in *Praise of Peace* and in *Praise of Folly* and Sir Thomas More's savage book *Utopia*. In the latter, despite the qualities that contemporary rulers found attractive in war, the high courage it called forth, the warmth of comradeship that soldiers cherished and the blowing away of materialist sloth which later philosophers, such as Hegel, found particularly valuable, Thomas More pointed out how deadly was the degradation it brought. In fact, More saw only the selfishness and evil which war could prompt in men, although the Utopians were men of their age in still wanting the things which could not be got without fighting and so they advocated the use of mercenaries to do their rulers' fighting for them.

[61]

Henry VIII's enthusiasm and preparedness for war were bound to have adverse effects on Anglo-Scottish relations. Two powerful and prideful rulers such as Henry and James could not be expected to be at ease with each other and it was only to be expected the less powerful would look for assistance elsewhere. The 'auld alliance' which had been broken by the Anglo-Scottish Treaty of 1502 had traditionally made France Scotland's best friend and strongest defence against English encroachment. In the circumstances James could well have seen the 1502 Treaty as an offence against sound statecraft. So when, in the run-up to Flodden, the French repeatedly called James' attention to their long-standing friendship with his country and urged him never to forget England's perfidy, they found an increasingly ready listener.[7]

On Henry's side, compared with his grand ambitions in Europe, Scotland was of far less interest but, unlike his father, he was not disposed to mollify the proud Scottish king. For instance, when Sir Robert Ker, the Scottish warden of the Middle March, was murdered by the Englishman, John Heron, during an official truce day, Henry made no attempt to punish Heron and he remained a free man.

Another source of grievance was the capture and death in 1511 of the Scottish sea-captain, Andrew Barton, by far the most notorious and successful of the Scottish privateers. Barton was highly regarded by the Scottish king and by the late spring of 1511 he had taken under his command a second ship, the *Jenny Pirwyn*, to join his famous 120-ton *Lyon*. Together they represented a genuine threat to English ships crossing to Europe and seemed to justify the many charges of piracy brought by the English against Barton. In June 1511 Henry commanded his Lord Admiral, Edward Howard, to end the menace. Andrew Barton was captured off the Downs; the English took his two ships as prizes and he died of the wounds received in the engagement. Predictably the Scots mounted furious protests which, by the treaty operating between them, Henry was obliged to consider together with any other grievances, but his contemptuous reply only worsened the situation. Henry not only told James that 'kings did not concern themselves with the affairs of pirates' but maintained that the treaty of 1502 had no application to the Barton case.[8]

In contrast with this studied disdain, the French supplied James with skilled shipwrights and allowed him to purchase timber suitable for shipbuilding, while at the same time putting forward proposals regarding the best ways of developing Scottish shipbuilding facilities in the Forth.

By 5 December 1511 relations between Scotland and England had deteriorated to such an extent that James wrote to the Pope asking him to free him from his treaty oaths on the grounds that Henry had waged both open and secret war against him.[9] Nevertheless in the following month James appeared still to harbour hopes of taking part in a projected crusade against the Turks, which would, of course, not take place if there was war between the major European powers. Such expectations were, in fact, quite unrealistic, for during the same month the English parliament voted a subsidy of two fifteenths to support Henry's projected invasion of France, and followed this by crassly resurrecting the English crown's claim to overlordship of Scotland by declaring the king of Scots 'very homager and obediencer of right to your highness'. A year or so later the Scottish and English kings' dislike for each other descended to spitefulness when Henry, concerned about his own succession and resenting the closeness of his sister, Margaret – James' wife – to the English throne, refused to pass over the treasure willed her by Henry VII. This brought a vigorous protest to the English ambassador from both Margaret and her husband during April 1513.[10]

In such a climate English attempts to avoid a full break with Scotland appeared unimpressive, if not half-hearted. When Henry VIII's uncharismatic ambassador to Scotland, Nicolas West, Dean of Windsor, was sent north he had nothing tangible to offer the Scottish king for keeping the peace.

For three weeks in April 1513 the Scots fobbed him off with vague promises and he left the country convinced it was about to pledge itself to France.

The Scottish king was indeed moving steadily into the French camp, but he had much to gain by delaying his official commitment for as long as possible. Accordingly the French continued their pressure during May 1513: Louis promised to supplement his offer of military support by agreeing to equip and victual the Scottish fleet and to deliver a large subsidy of 50,000 francs (£22,500 Scots), together with seven galleys commanded by the notable French admiral, Gaston Prégent de Bidoux. For this he demanded a high price: the Scottish king had not only to voice his disapproval of any English attack on France but to give an undertaking he would invade England as soon as Henry invaded France. In this event Louis promised to advance James' claims to the crown of England[11] – a vague enough promise but one guaranteed to infuriate and alarm Henry VIII. Typically, the French offer to equip and victual the Scottish fleet also had the further condition that in return James was obliged to send his fleet to France, if possible with additional Danish ships.[12]

Later in the same month the French played what they conceivably hoped was their ace card in clinching Scottish support, their appeal to James' well-known chivalrous nature. Queen Anne of France sent him a letter, accompanied by her turquoise ring and yet another subsidy of 14,000 crowns, appointing him as her chosen knight. Her appeal was couched in suitably piteous tones, 'She was a lady in a dolorous plight with the enemy at her door and as her bounden champion she laid it on James IV to march for her sake three feet onto English ground.'[13] Accompanying her letter came Louis' 'final' confirmation of military assistance together with a consignment of two cannons, 1000 handguns, 6000 eighteen-foot pikes, and a further gift of 25,000 crowns. A French knight, d'Aussi, acted as escort for the supplies and also brought with him professional captains who would train the Scottish troops in the latest methods of warfare.

With the English king proving not only capricious and insensitive but contemptuous, such offers gave the French their Scottish support. During May the the English admiral Sir Edward Howard, who had earlier killed Andrew Barton, was himself killed by the French while making a rash attack upon Admiral Prégent's galley in Brest harbour. In a communication to the English king, James ironically observed that the admiral's services would have been better employed against the enemies of Christ:[14] unsurprisingly, Henry made no reply. Nonetheless, in spite of his continuing preparations for war during late May, James was still going through the motions of attempting to save France from an English attack by urging the English king to reconsider his projected French expedition. His final communication offered to pardon all damage between them and renew the peace if Henry would undertake to maintain 'universal peace in Christendom'[15] – although there seemed little reason to think Henry would change his mind.

The final exchange between the Scottish and English kings prior to the Flodden campaign, came on 11 August 1513, one week before the Scottish main army set out for the border, when James' herald visited the English army in France close to their chosen objective, the town of Thérouanne. There he delivered an abusive ultimatum from his master, requiring Henry to 'desist from further invasion and utter destruction of our brother and cousin, the Most Christian King', and stating that 'we are bounden and obliged for mutual defence the one of the other . . . and we will do what thing we trust may cause you to desist from pursuit of him.'

Henry had already received reports from his spies that James' preparations to attack England were well advanced and he met threat with threat by first telling the herald that James was 'no competent judge of so high authoritie to require us in that behalfe'.[16] He then twisted the knife by repeating his claim of feudal superiority over Scotland, informing the herald that if his king dared to invade he would regret it: 'he shall have enough to do whensoever he beginneth and also I trusted him not so well but that I am provided for him right well and that shall he well know.'

However menacing such threats, neither Henry nor James appeared fully committed to a large military encounter in the rugged hill country of the eastern Marches. By far the greater part of English treasure had been lavished on the English king's quest to humble France where he enjoyed the declared, if ultimately shaky, support of not only the Pope but also the other main rulers in Europe. In comparison, Scotland was a lower priority and accordingly Henry allocated comparatively modest resources to meet the northern threat. In any case if, in accordance with his directions, Surrey placed the English northern levies in a good defensive position Henry believed the Scots would be unlikely to risk an outright battle.

James, the potential aggressor, despite having a large army and a notable artillery train at his back, also had his own good reasons to be cautious. The record of earlier Scottish armies crossing into England, like that under King David II at Neville's Cross in 1346, had been far from encouraging, while French support for his own small country had not always proved the boon expected. Not that long ago, in 1484–5, the French had coerced Scotland into what, from that country's point of view, had been a quite unnecessary war.

Even so, two determined and powerful kings opted to fight. In Henry's case this meant devoting massive resources to take on both mighty France and a resurgent Scotland, while James, with so little to gain, still placed his nation's future in jeopardy. Intriguingly, like so many other military campaigns, the outcome would not meet the expectations of either king.

PART TWO

Opposing Forces

CHAPTER FOUR

THE SOLDIERS AND
THEIR WEAPONS

It is not big armies that win battles; it is the good ones
Maurice de Saxe, *Mes Rêveries*

FROM EARLY 1513, both Scotland and England were actively preparing for war. While neither country had a standing army – Henry VIII's regular Yeoman of the Guard were 600 strong at most and the Scottish king lacked even that bodyguard – their preparations varied widely. Strategically things were much simpler for the Scots. They had one enemy, England, presently acting on the defensive against them. England on the other hand faced a fight with both France and Scotland and, in the circumstances, gave clear priority to the army scheduled for France rather than the northern levies appointed to guard a border more than 300 miles north of London.

During June 1513, the English assembled their main army of about 35,000 men at the ports of Dover, Hythe and Folkstone. Here they embarked on some hundreds of ships – so many that one eye-witness reported it was 'a sight such as Neptune had never seen before'[1] – and sailed to the port of Calais, England's last bridgehead in France, already placed on war alert. By the end of the month the whole superbly equipped force, including the king, were on French soil. For such overseas campaigning soldiers had to be engaged for months rather than the weeks or even days needed for border manoeuvrings. In the event Henry's French campaign was to last for almost six months and in such circumstances the English could not rely on the short-term commitment of their feudal array, even with extensions to its traditional forty-day period of service. In fact, since the late thirteenth century and the reign of Edward I, a good proportion of English troops had been customarily paid and indentures or private contracts were struck with individual nobles and their followers, while ordinary levies who served beyond their obligatory period also received pay. Assembling such an army was therefore an enormously expensive undertaking, made more costly still by Henry VIII's determination to hire heavy cavalry and pikemen.

Mercenary cavalry were needed to face the French heavy horse for, since their humiliation at Bannockburn, most English nobles had ceased to fight on horseback. From England's own resources Henry probably had about 3000 light cavalry, both 'javelins' and 'demi-lances' (general terms describing half-armoured men on unprotected horses), together with a number of 'border prickers' on small, wiry mounts primarily for use in skirmishing or scouting. His heavy cavalry were hired from the Netherlands and were known as Burgundians, so-called by the Emperor Maximilian as they originated from the 'Burgunder Kreis', the circle of Burgundy which came under his control following his marriage to Mary of Burgundy.[2]

English foot soldiers consisted of the old-style bill and bowmen (although there were some pikemen serving in France with the Duke of Buckingham and the lords Lyle and Abergavenny).[3] While not expected to match pikemen, in the right circumstances billmen could well hold their own against cavalry. Their bills had been adapted from an agricultural tool used originally for hedging: about eight feet long, the head was part axe and hook, topped by a spike. In practised hands its hook could unhorse a cavalryman, the spike thrust into his less well protected areas and the blade smash against and cut into body armour.

As for their archers, the English still considered their longbow most effective. Henry VII had earlier appointed commissions of a president (usually a noted territorial magnate), half a dozen stout gentlemen and the sheriff[4] to raise the set numbers of such men required from each shire. In any case facilities for developing archery skills existed in every town and village and as an excellent bowman Henry VIII set an example. The longbow's range, penetrative power and rate of fire equalled any comparable weapon in the world and the English had long ensured they had plenty of bow staves by requiring all overseas merchants to carry a quota with each cargo of imported goods.[5] By 1513 English archers also carried quivers, portable arsenals holding twenty-four or more arrows.

However, for his army bound for France, Henry VIII was not content to rely on his billmen and bowmen alone. After their reverses against the English in the previous century, the French could no longer be relied upon to make frontal assaults on English defensive lines. To better meet the variable tactics developed by the heavy French cavalry, Henry hired pikemen from Germany and Switzerland, Almaynes and Landsknechts, bearing sixteen- to eighteen-foot weapons. Two thousand of these supplemented the king's division, and a further 2500 accompanied his vanguard. In fact they were not called upon, since during the king's 1513 campaign none of his pikemen clashed with the French cavalry.

In accordance with its other lavish weaponry the royal army in France was supported by a strong artillery train under Sir Sampson Norton, the king's master of the ordnance. Specifically this consisted of ten massive cannon (for siege operations), eleven demi-cannon, twenty-one culverins, fourteen demi-culverins, twenty sakers, thirteen falcons, five bombards and one cannon perrier. In terms of projectiles, a cannon could fire an amazing 60lb shot, a demi-cannon one of 30lb with a missile roughly the size of a large grapefruit, a culverin up to 18lb shot, and demi-culverins, sakers and falcons rounds of 9, 5 and 2.5lb respectively.

As Henry pinned his hopes for military glory on his French campaign it followed that he would allot the pick of his ordnance to it, guns that required an amazing 1300 carriages and 1900 men to service them. It is fair to say that Henry stinted on nothing. Among his personal entourage was his almoner (Thomas Wolsey), accompanied by '115 members of his chapel, minstrels, players, heralds, trumpeters, clerks of the signet and privy seal, over three hundred other members of the Household, two bishops, a duke and a score of other nobles, together with an abundance of royal clothing and jewellery, and a huge bed.'[6]

North of the border the Scots also called together an impressive host. It was not only the largest army they had ever assembled but it was as well equipped as any other in Scottish history, for in accordance with the weapons policy developed by the James kings it had a most impressive artillery train. Within its ranks were nearly all the Scottish peerage who, with their practised and long-standing retainers, made up a sizeable proportion of the total.

The Scottish system of calling out all men between sixteen and sixty for feudal rather than paid service dated from medieval times, and although no one could deny the warlike nature of the Scots when fighting in their country's defence, the majority served for only a forty-day liability for which they were expected to bring sufficient food with them. On campaign such rations were liable to run short, after which the soldiers would be looking for whatever food they could pick up in addition to other plunder. Such a system meant the king had to wait until the last moment before sending out his summonses, and the shorter the notice the less time his army would have for unit training.

Due to this rudimentary system of mobilisation, and because the treasurers' accounts from August 1513 to June 1515 are missing, the exact size of the Scottish host is uncertain. An additional difficulty here is the considerable differences between the numbers of men who answered their king's call and mustered both outside Edinburgh and at Ellem Kirk, near the border, and those who eventually took part in the main battle. Such differences are not so marked with the English northern army, for the vast majority of those who assembled close to Alnwick went on to fight and in any case we have firmer evidence as to the army's actual numbers.

Estimated Strengths of the Scottish and English Armies at Flodden

	Source	Scottish Troops	English Troops
	Edward Hall	100,000	26,000
	The Trewe Encountre	100,000	26,000
Reports made close to the time of battle	*Articles of Battle* (Official despatch by Sir Thomas Howard to Henry VIII)	80,000	26,000 approx
	Brian Tuke (in a letter to Richard Pace)	60,000	30,000
	Polydore Vergil	60,000	30,000
Other 16th-century commentators	Buchanan	15,000	26,000
	Pitscottie	30,000	16,000
English 18th-century writer	Ridpath	60–100,000	26,000
1st half 20th century	W.M. Mackenzie	over 15,000	15,000
	R.L. Mackie	over 20,000	20,000
2nd half 20th century	Featherstone	40,000	less than 30,000
	Kightly	40,000	26,000 maximum

The greatest variations in the size of the two armies occur with the earliest observers who were either there or reputedly took their evidence from eye-witnesses. Both Edward Hall and the *Trewe Encountre* make the Scots' numbers far greater and Sir Thomas Howard also gives them a superiority of well over 2:1, as did Brian Tuke (English clerk of the Signet) in his letter to Richard Pace soon after the battle. With respect to such totals it is entirely possible that a despatch from an English commander to Henry VIII might tend to paint a picture in the sender's own favour, while Edward Hall and the writer of the *Trewe Encountre*, like other chroniclers before them, could possibly have inflated the number (on both sides) to make the battle more dramatic. Even so, they are consistent in giving the Scots a massive numerical superiority.

Of the later sixteenth-century commentators the Scots writer Pitscottie reduced the totals while still giving his countrymen a near 100% superiority, while the proud and fiercely patriotic Scottish historian George Buchanan, contradicting all the other commentators whether before or after him, actually gives the English a numerical advantage, and put it at an amazing 50%. On the other hand Polydore Vergil, the more dispassionate Italian historian who spent much of his time in England, gave the Scots an advantage of 2:1, as during the next century did George Ridpath, the English border historian.

In the last century a thorough-going and careful analysis undertaken by two Scottish historians, namely the iconoclastic William MacKay Mackenzie (who in his earlier study of Bannockburn also much reduced the size of the armies on both sides) and R. L. Mackie, resulted in them giving the Scottish forces an unstated but comparatively small advantage. In his examination of the English army Mackie quotes Surrey's submission to the king with regard to those who dispersed after the battle, specifying a body of 18,689 men, numbers that did not include the artillerymen nor, understandably, those lost on the battlefield. From such 'hard facts' the English army at Flodden was very likely to have been 20-22,000 strong before the battle, but somewhat higher if its casualties during the conflict were more than 1500–2000.[7]

Finally, two English authors, Donald Featherstone and Charles Kightly, writing in the later twentieth century, not only make the Scottish forces larger than the English but increase the differential between the two armies to more than 25%.

In summary, although there can be no doubt James IV

assembled a large and impressive force at the outset of the
Flodden campaign, with units from throughout Scotland, we
know it had dwindled, for reasons which will be examined later,
by the time of the main battle. There, despite the figures of the
contemporary commentators, it was unlikely to have enjoyed
more than a 30% numerical superiority and it could have been
less still. Whatever the armies actual sizes, other factors such
as the two sides' ordnance, their small arms, other equipment
and their state of training, unit cohesiveness and, above all,
their respective leaders, would prove to be equally or more
significant.

With regard to artillery, although the English had a slightly
higher number of guns, that was the sum total of their superiority: with their most powerful guns in France, the Scots
ordnance enjoyed clear advantages. In his post-battle report,
Thomas Howard listed seventeen of the twenty Scottish pieces
that left Edinburgh, 'state of the art' weapons made of toughened brass[8] – that were superior to iron guns and also lighter
in weight. The three heaviest and most ungainly Scottish
cannons had probably been left somewhere along the line
of march, maybe at Norham or Etal, or just conceivably on
Flodden Hill. As a fighting man Howard was most compli-
mentary about them, praising their graceful proportions, small
touch-holes and high quality finish.[9] More important than their
appearance, however, was their battle potential, their weight
of shot, range and rate of fire. Among them were five great
fieldpieces conceivably capable of firing missiles up to 60lb,
but possibly no more than 36lb, two culverins – longer guns,
firing 10–20lb shot, four culverins pikmoyenne (the equivalent
of English sakers) firing 6–7lb shot and six culverins moyenne,
capable of firing shot of 4–5lb weight.[10] For sixteenth-century
ordnance the ranges of the Scottish guns were impressive. In
the case of the heavy weapons (from 10 to 60 pounders) their
point-blank range was 350 yards with an extreme range of
1950 yards; with the medium ordnance of 4½–9 pounders,
point blank range was 300 yards and extreme range around

1500 yards. With the heavy ordnance, overheating had to be taken into consideration, restricting their rate of fire to between 30–40 shots a day, while the medium ordnance were able to fire as often as they could be loaded.

In contrast the English artillery sent to Scotland consisted of five brass serpentines and eighteen falcons. The serpentines, no larger than the lightest Scottish ordnance, fired a 4–5lb ball from 300 yards point-blank range to an extreme one of 1500 yards, while the very light falcons fired a ball of no more than 2lb, with their respective point-blank and extreme ranges being 250 yards and 2000 yards.

In any direct dual the English guns would not be expected to last long, although they would benefit from their greater 'handiness', for the Scots' five great cannons and two culverins (their famous seven sisters likely to have been made by the king's master smelter in Edinburgh) were undoubtedly difficult to move both towards and on the battlefield. Together with their wooden carriages each would have weighed up to four tons. For this reason little imagination is needed to realise why the Scots decided to leave in Edinburgh their famous great cannon 'Mons Meg', made of iron and fully fifteen feet long, which with its carriage weighed nearly seven tons,[11] together with three other heavy cannon somewhere along their line of march. Each heavy cannon not only needed a team of thirty-two oxen and nine drivers – their being relatively few heavy horses in Scotland – but a platoon of pioneers to precede it flattening ruts and filling in potholes. The smaller Scottish ordnance would have needed fewer draught animals; sixteen oxen and one horse have been estimated as sufficient for the culverins,[12] and because of their creditable rate of progress from Edinburgh to Coldstream there is a distinct possibility that James IV used horses with his lighter gun teams. Notwithstanding, when the guns had to be dragged off road the problems posed by the rough and predominately soft ground of the border regions were likely to have been enormous. It was here that the English enjoyed clear advantages. All their guns and carriages were pulled by horses that were quicker and less clumsy than oxen, so when close to their intended place of firing they could be manhandled into position. It was probably with such manhandling in mind that the English brought with them more gunners, nearly 400 men to the Scots' 300 or so. Moreover, although the English guns might be 'pea-shooters' compared with the Scottish blunderbusses, they could be fired more quickly.

Whatever the theory, at Flodden neither side's artillery was manned by its best teams – a circumstance easily understandable as far as the English were concerned but somewhat surprising in the case of the Scots. Although the Scottish artillery continued to be commanded by James' master gunner, Robert Borthwick, his professional German gunners were away with the Scottish fleet and consequently they had to be replaced by comparatively inexperienced men. The English were without Sir Norton Sampson, their master of the ordnance, who accompanied his king in France, with the result that Sir Nicholas Appleyard, normally clerk of the ordnance, was put in overall charge, with William Blackenall, another clerk of the ordnance, serving as his master gunner.[13]

Fortunately for the English, in spite of such new leaders they retained a good core of experienced men as both gunners and matrosses – the later being less skilled than the 'tradesmen' gunners.

Considerable variations existed in the training and equipment of the two sides. The Scottish army, recruited not only from middle Scotland but from the Borders and Highlands, presents much the more complex picture. From the time of William Wallace and particularly under the inspired direction of Robert Bruce, the majority of Scottish soldiers were accustomed to fight in their hedgehog formations of spearmen, termed schiltrons, bodies that owed a considerable debt to the Greek phalanxes. However, following Bruce's successful use of them at Bannockburn in 1314 they were to suffer repeated reverses against England in battles such as Dupplin

Moor (1332), Halidon Hill (1333), Neville's Cross (1346) and Homildon Hill (1402).

This presented James IV with a major problem, namely how to take full advantage not only of his Lothian levies, but of the unique but differing martial qualities of his Borderers and Highlanders. The Borderers, astride their 'handy' ponies, had long proved their skills at reconnaissance and skirmishing, the traditional hit-and-run tactics of the border. They were undoubtedly well protected; many of their helmets gave additional safety by extending backwards by means of articulated neck-pieces, their torsos were covered by custom-built jackets with interwoven steel plates; their arms were encased in chain mail and stout leather riding boots stretched up to their thighs. For weapons they carried an eight-foot lance, a sword and a latch (a small hand-wound crossbow). The Highlanders, who were at their best on foot, were less well protected, but when swinging their long claymores (their traditional two-handed swords) it was virtually impossible for their opponents' hand weapons to get through to them. Many also carried shortbows. Such men were unquestionably happiest moving forward on the attack.

During the uneasy months preceding the Flodden campaign the Scottish king was likely to have held a series of meetings with his subordinate leaders about how best to meet an English army and during their discussions it would have become clear that certain options were denied them. Like earlier Scottish commanders they could, for instance, never assemble a respectable body of heavy cavalry – there were few suitable horses in Scotland and they lacked the resources to hire additional ones. It was the same with longbowmen: most of the Scottish archers who traditionally came from the area of Ettrick Forest were no match for the English in range and hitting power. In any case, prolonged efforts had failed to persuade Scots to forsake football in favour of developing archery skills.

Apart from maximising the power of his formidable artillery, James was likely to have concluded that the best way to beat the English lay in improving the performance of his schiltrons, and various measures had already been taken in this direction. To blunt the effects of the dreaded English arrows, many of the nobles who traditionally occupied the front ranks were encouraged to acquire 'almain armour', i.e. plate armour of a riveted design either bought from Europe or manufactured by French armourers at a harness mill in Stirling. Many had responded, and by 1513 when equipped in a complete harness of plate armour, including arm defences, they could face longbowmen with new confidence, for an arrow could only be sure to penetrate if it struck square on. Others in the front ranks equipped themselves with large wooden shields, or pavises, that measured over four feet high as further protection against arrows (these were normally discarded when they closed with the enemy for hand-to-hand fighting).

For the Scottish king, however, the predominant question related to the tactical role of his schiltrons. From Scots who had fought on the Continent James must have learned of the formation's formidable competitors, such as the phalanxes of Swiss pikemen which, from 1470 onwards, had devastated opposing formations, including heavy cavalry, and had been used extensively not only in the French but also in the Spanish and Papal armies. In 1480, for instance, the French king, Louis XI, had 6000 Swiss soldiers in his service whose numbers had grown to 8000 when he invaded Italy in 1494. They carried pikes between sixteen and eighteen feet long and they were exceedingly well trained to fight in dense columns of men packed shoulder to shoulder, with four to five rows of pikes projecting beyond the front rank. They were further protected by halberdiers, men armed with six-foot axes, who preceded the column when it was on the move or screened its vulnerable flanks when it was stationary. By the time of Flodden, however, the halberdiers were beginning to give way to haguebuts, i.e. men carrying heavy hand guns. From 1486 onward the Swiss had to compete against rivals from the Hapsburg states whose landsknects, or pike-armed infantry, copied the Swiss methods of warfare and like the Swiss used specialist soldiers to give the pike columns greater protection. To their front went Doppelnsolders (men given double pay) whose great two-handled swords carved gaps in the opposing ranks for the pikemen to exploit, while to protect their flanks they used arquebusers (handgunners).

In Scotland attempts to improve the schiltrons' offensive powers were by no means new. In 1474 the Scottish parliament passed an act that no spears should be made shorter than 18 feet 6 inches, and this was repeated in 1481, although the length was later reduced to a not insignificant 17 feet 6 inches. Legislation was one thing, but to re-equip the schiltrons was a costly undertaking and with James IV's heavy expenditure on artillery and shipping little was significantly achieved until 1513 when long spears, together with other armaments, were shipped into Scotland from Holland.[14] Quite the most important tactical development, however, was the despatch from France of assorted military equipment, including 6000 long spears, accompanied by the knight called d'Aussi with fifty men-at-arms and forty veteran captains to help him train the Scots in their use.[15] The stores carried by d'Aussi failed to reach the Scottish forces before Flodden but d'Aussi himself, together with his instructors, successfully made their way to join them, probably before the full muster was completed on Edinburgh's Burghmuir. Despite the king's great faith in such French instructors – reputedly 'greater confidence than in God'[16] – they were given insufficient time to drill the schiltrons in handling such clumsy weapons. Nor were the Scottish columns screened by crossbowmen or by Highlanders whose claymores could have cleared their paths. Even so, James IV was so confident in the offensive capability of his pike columns that he ordered many of his Borderers to join them. The one formation not equipped with pikes were his Highlanders – whom he knew would surely have hated them.

With a fine artillery train and the bulk of his soldiers organised in their Swiss formations James might have felt he had done all he could to move the battlefield odds in his favour. He was, of course, not to know that the high noon of Swiss military supremacy was about to end at the battle of Marignano in 1515[17] and that the further development of artillery would make packed ranks of men increasingly vulnerable. In any case, with Henry VIII in France, James IV realised he was facing English levies from the northern counties who had no heavy cavalry nor pikemen of their own.

As for the English levies, although Niall Barr reckoned that 'the English army which fought at Flodden looked decidedly second rate and behind the times', the reality was some-what different. The Tudor system of mobilisation had worked smoothly enough after the king had placed the Earl of Surrey in charge of the country's defence 'should trouble come from the Scots'.[18] Indeed, by 1 August 1513 Surrey, who was at Lambeth, was bringing together and paying an element of experienced soldiers, and before long he had a retinue of 500, including five captains, five petty captains, one spear, forty-three demi-lances and 446 soldiers. To this he added a quasi-headquarters staff consisting of a marshal of the army, master of the ordnance, treasurer of the wars and a pursuivant (state messenger) as well as trumpeters, craftsmen and ser-vants.[19] An additional allowance of 4/- each was granted to such men in order to dress them in the king's livery.

After the Scots raided the border, Surrey ordered a general mobilisation of the northern levies, while more seasoned sol-diers were expected to join him from the Continent under his son, Thomas Howard, together with others among Sir Edward Stanley's large body of retainers. By the end of July Surrey had reached Pontefract with the nucleus of an army, and not much more than a month later the whole force was assembled and ready for action.

The speed with which the English gathered was impressive but, however efficient Surrey's mobilisation and the additional strength provided by his professional soldiers, the vast majority were a combination of levies and tenants from the estates of

Surrey's sub-unit commanders. The bows and bills carried by 80% of them were not considered adequate to face European armies, while Surrey's mounted arm was restricted to his light border horse totalling 1800 at most. However, unlike most of the Scottish Borderers, they were acting in the role they knew best. Yet nothing could change the fact that the English army was outnumbered, albeit not greatly, and unquestionably heavily outweaponed. In the Scottish pike columns it was facing a success-ful military formation and, even if the drilling carried out by their French trainers was superficial, Scottish soldiers were well used to adopting such an arrangement in their traditional schiltrons.

Conversely, the undeniably old-fashioned weapons of the English had certain virtues. Amateur soldiers or not, the bow-men amongst them came from a long and proud tradition, with skills developed through years of practice in their local butts and through regular competitions. The billmen would have practised their weapons at the periodic 'wappenshaws' required by Henry VIII, although, for that matter, any countryman used to wielding an axe, a pitchfork, or any other agricultural implement of the day, was capable of using his bill effectively, particularly against opponents whose hands might be occupied by long and clumsy pikes. Customary tactics accompanied such traditional weapons; the archers were deployed on the flanks to give protective fire both for the billmen and dismounted men-at-arms standing in lines four or five deep. Once the enemy joined battle the archers were practised in falling back and taking up their secondary weapons, such as swords, knives and even mallets, before rejoining the struggle. Such simple and familiar practices were not likely to break down even in the heat of battle, and as paid soldiers they were bound to be less con-cerned than their opponents with the prospects of plunder.

However important the respective force strengths, their contrasting weapon systems and opposing tactics, it was their performance on the day of battle that would prove decisive. This was, of course, the responsibility of their commanders, who are the subjects of the following two chapters.

CHAPTER FIVE

≈

THE ENGLISH COMMANDERS

United and activated by some common impulse of
passion, or of interests
James Madison, *The Federalist No 10*

RESPONSIBILITY FOR THE direction of the English forces
that gathered to meet the anticipated Scottish invasion
lay in the hands of a single eminent family – the Howards.
With Henry VIII in France the veteran Thomas Howard, Earl
of Surrey and second duke of Norfolk, held the dual posts of
lieutenant-general of the North and commander-in-chief. Surrey decided he must have a second-in-command who was not
only competent and energetic, but one whom he could trust
implicitly. He therefore asked for, and was granted, the services
of his eldest son, Thomas Howard, at that time Lord Admiral
of the English Navy, whom he also appointed as his vanguard
commander. Surrey gave the command of the vanguard's right
wing to another Howard, Thomas' younger brother Edmund.
While during the course of the battle others, such as the
Stanleys, Lord Dacre and Sir Marmaduke Constable would
hold important commands, overall control rested with Surrey
and his eldest son.

Thomas Howard, earl of Surrey and 2ⁿᵈ duke of Norfolk

By the time of Flodden, Surrey was not only England's most
experienced soldier but an old man of seventy. Although crippled
with arthritis which sometimes forced him to accompany his
troops in a cart, both his mental faculties and his urge to
succeed remained strong. The Scots made fun of his physical

problems but in spite of them he represented a formidable opponent. The Howards were an East Anglian family who, through one of their many advantageous marriages, inherited the dukedom of Norfolk, with Surrey's father the first in line. Surrey's own virility gave him a full quiver in the marriage stakes: by his first wife he fathered eight sons and three daughters – although three of the sons died young – and a further three sons and four daughters by a second marriage. The sons helped to maintain the family's military reputation: apart from Thomas, the eldest, and his younger brother, Edmund, who were, of course, with Surrey at Flodden, another brother, Edward, had already held the post of Lord Admiral until his death on 25 April 1512.

During Surrey's long and active public life he performed military and diplomatic services for a succession of monarchs. Forty-two years before Flodden he fought beside Edward IV at the Battle of Barnet and campaigned with him in France. For such faithful service he was not only made Earl of Surrey, but created a Knight of the Garter and became lord steward of the king's household and a member of his privy council. As a courtier Surrey distinguished himself by giving his complete loyalty to the wearer of the crown, whoever it might be. In this respect he acquiesced in Richard III's usurpation of Edward's throne and carried the sword of state at his coronation.

In 1485 both Surrey and his father fought at Bosworth Field for the reigning king, Richard III, although his father was killed and he himself was taken prisoner. For opposing Henry Tudor he was attainted, lost all his estates and was imprisoned in the Tower, where he remained for three and a half years, during which time the earl of Lincoln invaded England and offered Surrey his freedom if he would join him. True to his policy of supporting the reigning sovereign, Surrey refused and opted to remain where he was. The rebellion was quickly crushed and Henry VII, realising that Surrey not only had the ability to be a useful servant but to act as an example to less faithful nobles, released him in 1489. Henry was also unlikely to forget

Surrey's uncompromising reply when he was asked why he had continued to support Richard III at Bosworth: '[Because] he was my crowned King and if Parliamentary authority of England set the crown on a stock, I will fight for that stock. And as I fought then for him, I will fight for you.'[1] In this way Surrey safeguarded his large and growing family but he needed to perform effectively and, although not always easy, subordinate his own inclinations to those of his current royal master. Surrey was restored to his earldom, but the calculating Henry VII retained part of his estates.

Surrey quickly demonstrated his ability by successfully putting down a northern uprising and having the insurgents' leader hanged at York, for which he was rewarded by being made lieutenant-general of the North and sub-warden of the vulnerable east and middle Marches, with the young Arthur, Prince of Wales, as the nominal warden.[2] In 1492 Surrey's swift suppression of a rising at Acworth, near Pomfret, brought him recognition as Henry VII's chief general in England, and in this capacity his main responsibilities were guarding the Scottish border against a possible invasion by James IV and his protégé, Perkin Warbeck. Inevitably this gave him a thorough acquaintance with those regions and, in 1497, he advanced against the Scottish king and compelled him to break off his siege of Norham Castle. At Ayton, five miles north of Berwick, James IV challenged him to battle or to a single contest hand-to-hand, and although Surrey appeared to accept, James suddenly withdrew.[3] By 1501 Surrey was Henry VII's lord treasurer, in which capacity he went north to arrange a peace between England and Scotland which was to be confirmed by the marriage of Henry VII's daughter, Margaret, to James IV.

In 1503 he conducted the princess to Edinburgh where he was received with honour and apparently got on so well with the Scottish king that a petulant Margaret told her brother that, 'My Lord of Surrey is in [so] great favour with the King here that he cannot forebear the company of him no time of the day.'[4] Five years later Surrey was in Antwerp negotiating another royal marriage, this time between Henry VII's daughter, Mary, and Charles, Prince of Castille.[5] For such faithful service his manors were finally restored to him and, with his modest personal tastes, he had become a favourite of both the king and queen.

On Henry VIII's accession, Surrey's seniority and experience entitled him to be a leading adviser. Accordingly, in 1509, he was one of the commissioners who concluded a treaty with France, and in 1510 he became Earl Marshal. However, the ascetic and serious courtier of sixty-seven believed he was overtaken in the king's favour by the young, flamboyant and undoubtedly capable Thomas Wolsey. Surrey suspected Wolsey of fostering Henry VIII's high-flung ambitions in foreign affairs, contrary to the more cautious policy of Henry VII. In his frustration at the pattern of events Surrey gave way to outbursts of temper and, in September 1512, 'being discountenanced by the King he left the court.'[6] Wolsey rightly saw Surrey as a deadly rival and never lost an opportunity to poison Henry's mind against him, even recommending that he be barred from his lodgings at court, but Henry refused, for he was shrewd enough to appreciate Surrey's loyalty and his use as a possible counter-weight to his ambitious chancellor.

Nonetheless Wolsey succeeded in excluding Surrey from the expected glories of the king's French campaign when, as the long-time lieutenant-general of the North, he was made responsible for the English levies facing an anticipated Scottish attack. In fact Wolsey appeared to have placed him in a 'no win' situation, for Henry attached far more importance to continental war than he did to war with Scotland. It was in Europe where the laurels could be won. Surrey, like all good soldiers, knew this and wanted to be with the king. As for Scotland, the king was fully aware of the limitations of Surrey's armament and the formidable opposition he would face. He therefore expected him to adopt a defensive strategy and the conquest of Scotland was never contemplated.

Whether for the best reasons or not, the king chose well, for Surrey had repeatedly demonstrated his military efficiency and he had a deep knowledge of the border areas. In spite of his seventy years he was still capable of acting decisively. His was no easy task; the levies had to be moulded into effective formations and even when this was achieved the Scots could still be expected to have more men and much superior artillery.

Thomas Howard, later earl of Surrey and 3rd duke of Norfolk

Thomas Howard's career would eventually prove as long and remarkable as his father's, for he was still an important public figure in the reign of Mary Tudor. Unlike his strapping brother Edward, Thomas was 'small and spare of stature'[7] with black hair and, like Surrey, the only *sine qua non* of his behaviour appeared to be unquestioning loyalty to his sovereign and family. With this Howard the family's interests would increasingly be seen to coincide with his own. The concern of this book however is with the forty-year-old commander, not the later 'cold-hearted time-server, sadly fallen from the promise of the gallant young man who had fought Andrew Barton and charged home at Flodden.'[8]

At Flodden Thomas Howard demonstrated the qualities which made men follow him under adverse conditions. He was fit, energetic and confident, capable of making rapid decisions but also willing to listen to others. His soldiers apparently seldom saw him ruffled and he was always ready for a simple joke. Yet in spite of this, his achievements before Flodden had been comparatively modest. While his father was out of grace his early years were probably spent with his mother, but even when his father campaigned in the Scottish Marches at various times between 1489 and 1509 there is little mention of his eldest son, although he undoubtedly accompanied him on at least two occasions. Admittedly, in 1497 Thomas and his younger brother, Edward, were both knighted in the field, although they did not appear to have particularly distinguished themselves for such an honour. In 1503 Thomas was part of his father's retinue that accompanied Margaret Tudor for her betrothal to James IV, although with no direct role to play.

Five years before, Thomas had followed Howard practice by making an advantageous match of his own, to Lady Anne Plantagenet, daughter of Edward IV and sister-in-law to Henry VII. It proved far from successful. Thomas seemed to have little in common with Anne and he constantly quarrelled with his jealous and vindictive, if highly accomplished, wife. The match also failed in that none of their children survived into adulthood.

In military affairs he had been eclipsed by his younger brother, Edward, much closer in age to the young king and who became his standard bearer. During the frequent jousts that followed Henry VIII's coronation, the skills of both Thomas and Edward attracted attention. Thomas showed himself the better soldier and shrewder judge of the two, but Edward's gallant presence, remarkable strength and dare-devil qualities stood him higher in the king's estimation.

In 1511 Edward was made Lord Admiral of the fleet and gained great acclaim when he captured the notorious Scottish privateer, Andrew Barton (who subsequently died of the wounds sustained in the action), while Thomas was obliged to take part in Henry VIII's abortive campaign to assist Ferdinand against France. Edward's success was Henry VIII's first military triumph and it helped increase the king's regard for the Howards, particularly during 1512–13 when Edward kept the French fleet trapped in Brest. However, tiring of the blockade, Edward set out in a small boat, accompanied by three barges, to attack the assembled French fleet directly. It was an extremely rash undertaking and Edward was killed. Upon his death Thomas was appointed Lord Admiral.

In the short period before Flodden Thomas had little chance to impress the king by gaining immediate revenge on the

[88]

French navy but, in spite of having to act as a ferryman shipping the English army to the Continent,[9] he soon showed abilities that suggested he would be a worthy successor.[10] Whatever his naval prospects, it was the Flodden campaign that finally gave Thomas Howard the chance to show his undoubted qualities and to prove that 'when he fought [he could operate] with terrifying efficiency.'[11]

Edmund Howard

The English vanguard's right wing at Flodden was placed under Thomas' younger brother, Edmund, with its ranks stiffened by 500 of the admiral's professional soldiers. At one stage Edmund's appointment might not have seemed that advantageous, as more than half his force were less than happy at being commanded by someone who did not come from the Stanleys, their superior house. However, under the heaviest of attacks Edmund, too, demonstrated his family's traits of courage and tenacity.

Sir Edward Stanley

After the Howards, the Stanleys were the most prominent family at Flodden. They were predominantly from Lancashire and Cheshire but had representatives in the other northern counties, where one of their traditional duties was to guard the Isle of Man against the Scots. The Stanleys' large estates enabled them to bring at least 6500 men of their own and all, whether under Sir Edward Stanley or his brother James, the Bishop of Ely, apparently wore the bishop's badge of an eagle's foot with the bishopric's three crowns beneath it. The fighting bishop shared his episcopal residence with a lady by whom he sired at least two sons and a daughter, the eldest son, John, fighting beside him at Flodden.

[89]

Sir Edward Stanley was his family's most successful representative in the campaign. Like Surrey and Sir Marmaduke Constable he was of mature years, although his father, the Earl of Derby, was still alive and campaigning with the king in France. Like the other two, Edward Stanley had served Edward IV, even acting as a pall-bearer at the king's funeral, but with his father married to Henry Tudor's mother, the family came into strong favour on Henry VII's accession and Edward became involved in the major court ceremonials. In 1485 he was appointed sheriff of Lancashire with duties that included safeguarding the shire against possible Scottish attacks, and was later made Commissioner of Array for Yorkshire and Westmoreland. At Flodden, therefore, Stanley was performing a task not unfamiliar to him, and his shrewd use of ground and sound tactics proved him a distinguished rearguard commander. The popular ballad 'Flodden Field' emphasised his military reputation by recounting how the English army begged Surrey to place Stanley in command of the vanguard.[12] Surrey had, of course, already earmarked the post for his eldest son but, by appointing Stanley as rearguard commander, he was acknowledging his ability. Not only did Stanley surprise the opposing troops nearest him but the reputation he gained at Flodden was such that he was reported – mistakenly, as it turned out – to have killed the Scottish king by his own hand.

Sir Marmaduke Constable

While the Stanleys came from the north-west, the Constables were a powerful Yorkshire family whose seat of Flamborough on the north-east coast had been granted to them by Richard I during the twelfth century. Like Surrey and his eldest son, Sir Marmaduke was of small stature, being dubbed 'Little Sir Marmaduke'; a brass tablet presently in Flamborough church makes him seventy years old at the time of the battle (although this has been disputed). Whatever his age, he was reputedly still vigorous and, like Surrey, had much military experience, in both Britain and France under Edward IV and Henry VII, before mustering for Flodden with his powerful retinue.[13]

Like Surrey, Constable had taken part in previous diplomatic missions and immediately prior to the battle, as befitted such a distinguished subordinate, he signed the challenge from Surrey inviting the Scottish king to fight.

In many respects Marmaduke's formation and Sir Marmaduke himself (who before the admiral reordered the army, commanded the vanguard's left wing) epitomised the English army at Flodden. Its levies from Yorkshire's East Riding were serving under their family superiors and facing their traditional enemies. Constable's kinsmen included his son-in-law, William Percy, his brother, William Constable, along with his three sons, Sir Robert Constable, Marmaduke Constable and William Constable, together with John Constable of Holderness and other gentlemen from both Yorkshire and Northumberland. The fraternal quality of his formation was emphasised in a poetic description of the battle:

> Sir Marmaduke Constable stout
> Accompanied with his seemly sons
> Sir William Bulmer with his rout,
> Lord Clifford with his clapping guns.[14]

At Flodden things went well for Sir Marmaduke. Henry VIII personally acknowledged the services of the old warrior in a letter of thanks sent from Windsor, and his two sons, together with his brother and William Percy, were all knighted for their efforts.[15]

Lord Thomas Dacre of Gilsland

The other 'non-Howard' divisional commander, Dacre, came from a famous Border family which, over the years, was heavily involved in the fighting there. In the fourteenth and fifteenth centuries its representatives were made sheriffs of Cumberland, constables of Carlisle Castle and wardens of the western Marches. From May 1486, when just twenty-one years of age, Thomas Dacre was appointed lieutenant of the west Marches, until becoming deputy, and then full warden. In 1494 he fought at the siege of Norham Castle, but undoubtedly his most notable military responsibility came at Flodden where he was right rearguard commander before having his command reduced to his 1500 border horsemen.

Dacre was undoubtedly a vigorous soldier, despite suffering from gout, although the demanding Surrey was also fully conscious of his weaknesses. He subsequently wrote of him that 'there was no hardier or better knight but he neglects order.'[16] For his contribution at Flodden Dacre was granted more land on the borders, this time at Lanercost near the English western fortress of Carlisle.

At Flodden the English were directed by the experienced head of an ambitious military family, powerfully assisted by his son. Both father and son had the strongest personal reasons to succeed and they shared a single and undeviating aim, namely to bring their opponents to battle and to beat them. On Henry VIII's departure for France, Surrey bitterly regretted being left to deal with James, and his disappointment made him the more determined to teach James a lesson: 'Sory may I see hym or I dye, that is cause of my abydinge behynde and if ever he and I mete I shall do that in my lyeth to mak him as sory.'

For Thomas the campaign offered a unique chance to emerge finally as a leader in his own right. Under them were commanders and men from the north of England long experienced at fighting the Scots, who faced an invading army that had not only moved onto English soil but encamped there.

CHAPTER SIX

———————————— ≈ ————————————

THE SCOTTISH COMMANDERS

Better one bad general than two good ones
Napoleon

THE SCOTTISH HOST under the command of James IV was a national army in so far as any of that era could be said to be such. Scottish monarchs had especial difficulties here because their country was only just coming to accept that its true centre lay in Edinburgh. The Central Lowlands, Borders, Highlands and the islands still had their own interests, loyalties and traditions. Like elsewhere in Europe, the Scottish kings had attempted to break down these local divisions and to concentrate their territories. Nowhere was this easy to do and in Scotland the difficulties were much greater and longer-lasting than in England. If this had not been so it is doubtful whether even Edward I would have dreamed of conquering and annexing Scotland, for a united Scotland would surely have seemed beyond his resources.

Nonetheless, by the time of James IV a great deal of centralised royal power had been achieved. But the unity that even hard-hearted and heavy-handed Stewart kings could achieve needed time and in Scotland it was far from complete by the time of Flodden; for while the Jamesean line of Kings were consolidating their centralising authority the great nobles were attempting to build up their decentralised power bases.

Nobody, however, should underestimate the great advances in civility and wealth by the time of, and under, James IV. He had, for instance, massively reduced internal disputes over land ownership by introducing fixity of tenure; henceforth, the feuing (or letting) of land by both the king and others to third parties was to stand 'perpetually to their heirs'. Even more importantly, he had extended the convergent movements of his immediate predecessors, using Edinburgh as his capital and administrative centre, and bringing the outlying regions further under his control, even engaging Highland chieftains, including one-time rebels such as Matthew Stewart, Earl of Lennox, in his daily councils.

From 1504 royal justiciars and sheriffs had been appointed for the Western Isles, and in the same year he had brought under his control a number of the most powerful clans from the lawless border regions, such as the Jardines and the Armstrongs. These reforms, however, were relatively recent and the old barbarism and ingrained internal feuding were far from dead, although kept quiescent by a king skilled in balancing his magnates' respective ambitions. His policy of imposing forfeitures and then rapidly repealing them, for instance, had worked with John Ramsay, formerly Lord Bothwell, who, as late as 1496, advised Henry VII how to catch and beat the Scottish army, but was subsequently persuaded to switch his allegiance to James IV and died with him at Flodden.[1]

There was never any doubt the royal standard must fly at Flodden. It was James who called his peoples together and promised to teach the arrogant English king a much-needed lesson. By so doing he was putting at risk all his remarkable achievements but he would have had it no other way. He had not only gained his throne through success on the battlefield but from that time had been fascinated by military and naval weaponry, particularly artillery. He fancied himself as a Renaissance warrior prince and he was surely correct in thinking that only his presence on the field could hold together the heterogeneous posse that was his national army. He was certainly right in believing that the qualities of dash and derring-do which were so markedly his were also the qualities his people admired and most wanted to see in their leader.

The war he fought at Flodden turned out to be a medieval

one, yet in his appreciation of artillery and sea power it was modern war he was anticipating – a form of war needing resources beyond Scotland's capacity to supply at that time. Although sea power was so important to him he could for instance, never match the spending capacity of England on its navy.

James IV's problems were compounded by the achievements of Henry VII of England in that he completed the work of the Wars of the Roses and had brought to heel the great English feudatories. While James IV was temperamentally more adventurous and the more attractive king, because Scotland was at an earlier stage of consolidation he would have done well to model his statecraft more on Henry VII's than endangering all his achievements so far by spending his limited capital on war. Prior to making war he needed to strengthen his tightening grip on his peoples whose instinctive loyalty was still to local diverse interests and not, as yet, to the larger unifying ones. How terrifyingly strong the great noble families of Scotland were at the time of Flodden can be seen by the commanders' roll there.

Alexander, 3rd Lord Home

One of two leaders of the Scottish vanguard, Home was from one of the oldest and most famous border families originating with the earls of Dunbar and March, and connected with the princes of Northumberland and England's Saxon kings. The family's history is closely inter-linked with its extensive estates around Greenlaw in Berwickshire, from where it long guarded the Scottish eastern Marches against Northumberland. But during the frequent border clashes of the fourteenth century the family's feudal lords became noted for the frequency with which they changed sides between England and Scotland,[2] and the Homes, more consistent in their support of the

Scottish king, found themselves opposing the 10th earl of Dunbar and March at Homildon Hill; during this battle their chief, Sir Alexander Home, was taken prisoner and subsequently killed fighting as an auxiliary in France. After James I overthrew the earls of Dunbar and March in 1436 the Homes were granted some of their estates and themselves became wardens of the eastern Marches. The Home family's dramatic advancement was demonstrated in 1473 when its head, Sir Alexander Home, was both made a peer and entrusted by James III to head diplomatic missions to the English court.

During the fifteenth century the Home family's interests, like those of so many other Scottish magnates, clashed with those of their sovereign, James III. One of the family's traditional privileges was the hereditary office of baillie to the monastic lands of Coldingham, and Lord Home became incensed when, with the Pope's help, the king succeeded in transferring the revenues of Coldingham to his chapel royal at Stirling. With the king's eldest son and other disaffected nobles, Home rose in rebellion and his border spearmen played a considerable part in bringing about James' defeat at Sauchieburn.

On James IV's accession the Homes were rewarded for their support. They regained the revenues of Coldingham and Alexander not only obtained the office of Great Chamberlain of Scotland for life but resumed the wardenship of the eastern Marches; he was also made captain of Stirling Castle. Home's support for James IV was, however, not without its perils for, in 1497, after James invaded England with Perkin Warbeck, the English retaliated with Surrey laying waste to the Homes' estates and demolishing Ayton Castle, one of their strongest forts. James continued to support the Homes and prior to Flodden authorised the 3rd earl, Alexander, to lead a major raid into England, which turned out to be unsuccessful. Despite its failure the family was at the pinnacle of its power at this time.[3]

Alexander Gordon, 3rd earl of Huntly

Home's joint commander of the vanguard, and of its Highland contingents, Alexander Gordon, was from another of Scotland's great ruling families. Of Anglo-Norman descent, they were initially granted estates in Berwickshire in recognition of their support for David I, and as a notable warrior family subsequently featured in Scotland's many conflicts. James Taylor has written that 'They . . . shed their blood like water for their sovereign and country, at home and abroad, on the scaffold and the battlefield [they] earned distinction both as statesmen and warriors and have filled the highest offices in the Church and the State.'[4]

Taylor did not exaggerate the Gordons' devotion to the patriotic cause. During 1296 Adam de Gordon was killed during the first war of Independence but the family's opposition to the English continued through his son, Sir Adam de Gordon, who supported John Balliol and joined with William Wallace until his major defeat at Falkirk in 1298. After Balliol's death he transferred his loyalty to Robert Bruce and was one of Bruce's ambassadors who carried the Declaration of Arbroath, Scotland's pledge of national independence, to Rome; it was Bruce who deliberately moved the family's territorial interests northwards by granting them the barony of Strathbogie in Aberdeenshire. Adam de Gordon supported Bruce's son, King David II, at Halidon Hill in 1333 where he was killed. The family attained prominence again at the Battle of Neville's Cross (1346) where Sir John de Gordon was captured and not released until 1357.

After a further succession of encounters with the English, his son, also Sir John was killed at the Battle of Otterburn on 19 August 1388 and his descendant, Sir Adam Gordon, died at Homildon Hill on 14 September 1402. At Homildon Adam demonstrated the family's renowned bravery by joining with a border knight, Sir John Swinton (who had been at feud with the Gordons), to head one hundred horsemen who, in an attempt to turn the fortunes of the battle, galloped down the hill in the face of far superior numbers.[5] All were killed and Adam's only child, Elizabeth of Gordon, subsequently married Sir Alexander Seton, a Lothian magnate, who became head of the Gordons. James II appointed his son 1st earl of Huntly and he repaid the royal favour by fighting against rebellious Highland lords at Brechin on 18 May 1452. Two years later he went on to defeat the earls of Moray and Ormond, forcing them to take shelter in the Western Isles.

By now the family were unquestionably major northern landowners and George, 2nd earl of Huntly, was made joint justiciar for Scotland beyond the Forth. In 1488 he supported James III against his son at Sauchieburn where, with the Earl of Atholl, he commanded the king's vanguard. After James III's death the new king, anxious for the loyalty of such a formidable family, made George his lieutenant in northern Scotland beyond the River North Esk. In 1498 George was made chancellor of Scotland and, following his death four years later, Alexander, the 3rd earl, was prominent in helping James IV subdue the Western Isles again. Working in conjunction with the king's fleet, he led an attack on the island chieftains and by 1505 he had stormed the Castle of Stornoway held by Torquil Macleod, one of the principal western chiefs,[6] and forced Donald Dubh, claimant to the lordship of the Isles, to flee to Ireland; from that time the independent lordship of the Isles ceased to exist.[7] As a reward the king confirmed Alexander in his lands, including those of the Gordons, which were now termed the Barony and Earldom of Huntly and, on 24 October 1509, Alexander was appointed sheriff and keeper of Inverness Castle, with powers of jurisdiction over the counties of Inverness, Ross and Caithness.

Like the Homes, the Huntlys came to Flodden at the peak of their family's fortunes: according to Holinshed, Alexander was held 'in the highest reputation of all the Scottish nobility for his valour joined with this wisdom and policy'.[8]

Matthew Stewart, 2nd earl of Lennox

The Highland Division was led by two further representatives of Scotland's old ruling families. Matthew Stewart came from the branch of the fighting Stewarts founded by Sir Alan Stewart of Dreghorn, which gained a distinguished fighting reputation both in Scotland and France and, like other powerful families who survived the country's internal convulsions from the thirteenth century onwards, its leaders were jealous in defending their interests. The Stewarts accompanied Edward Bruce to Ireland where they took part in his military actions, but Sir Alan was subsequently killed with two of his brothers at the battle of Halidon Hill on 19 July 1333. From then on the Stewarts became celebrated for their fighting in France. In 1419 Sir John Stewart of Darnley was appointed as joint commander of the six thousand Scottish troops sent to assist the dauphin, later Charles VII of France, gain the French crown. In 1421 they beat an English army under Henry V's brother, Clarence, at Baugé where Clarence was killed, and for his role there Sir John received the lands of Concressault and later those of Aubigny-sur-Neve.[9]

Back in Scotland Sir John was succeeded by Sir Alan Stewart, and it was his son, John, who initiated the persistent and long-standing family claims to the earldom of Lennox. In 1463 he presented a charter to parliament putting forward his claim, and in 1471 he again attempted to obtain recognition of a share in the title. In 1465 James III made him governor of Rothesay Castle on the Isle of Bute and, while the king was confined in Edinburgh, Darnley attended him as warden of the West Borders. In 1482 James III declared Darnley and his followers to be his true lieges, but this nevertheless did not stop Darnley joining a conspiracy against the king in that same year.[10]

After the accession of James IV, Darnley was made keeper of Dumbarton Castle and sat as Lord Lennox in parliament but, disappointed at not being given more influential offices of state, he rebelled against the new administration, as a result of which his strongholds of Duchal and Crookston were taken and he was himself defeated at Tallymoss[11] on the south side of the Forth. Dumbarton Castle was then besieged on behalf of James IV by the Earl of Argyll, and soon surrendered. After making peace with James IV the act of forfeiture against him was rescinded on 5 February 1490 and Matthew Stewart, his son and 2nd earl of Lennox, who succeeded in 1494, finally obtained a charter for the Lennox earldom for both himself and his male heirs. Meanwhile, Sir John's other son, Robert Stewart of Aubigny, enjoyed a sparkling military career in France, first under Bernard Stewart, seigneur of Aubigny, and then in the Italian wars of 1500–13, which resulted in him being made a *maréchal* of France.

The later Stewarts of Darnley undoubtedly possessed great military talents, together with a restlessness, high pride and continuing sense of grievance that were mirrored by some other Highland families. James IV acknowledged both the family's prominence – and its potential to cause unrest – by quickly forgiving their rebellion against him and, along with Argyll, giving Matthew Stewart senior command at Flodden.

Archibald Campbell, 2nd earl of Argyll

Argyll came from a family that originated as lairds of Loch Awe about whom Taylor wrote, 'by dint of remarkable ability, shrewdness, energy and good fortune [they] not only absorbed . . . the smaller clans of Lorne . . . but have also ousted the once powerful clan Donald from the supremacy which they long held in the Western Islands.'[12] A Colin Campbell was chief of Loch Awe at the time of William the Lyon, but up to the end of the thirteenth century the family's most distinguished representative was the unrelentingly ambitious Colin Campbell, seventh clan chief, who was knighted by

Alexander III and who not only succeeded in making large acquisitions to his estate (as would later Campbells) but by his warlike actions acquired the surname of More or Great.[13] Henceforth, Campbell chieftains were given the Gaelic title of MacCalan More.

In 1291, Colin Campbell joined the Bruce cause by supporting the candidature of Robert Bruce (the Competitor) for the Scottish throne. His successor, Sir Niel Campbell, was said to have fought by Robert Bruces's (Robert I's) side in almost all his encounters from the battle of Methven to Bannockburn, and was one of the barons who participated in Bruce's great parliament at Ayr on 26 April 1315 when the future succession of the crown was settled. In 1316 his son, Sir Colin Campbell of Loch Awe, accompanied Robert Bruce to Ireland to assist his brother Edward to gain the Irish throne, and it was there an incident occurred that became the subject of a well-known story. In 1317 the king had given unequivocal orders that no one was to leave the ranks, but as the Scottish forces were passing through a wood two English archers discharged their arrows at Sir Colin and he could not resist giving chase. The king pursued him and struck him so violently with his truncheon that he was almost unhorsed, before commanding him to return to the ranks, shouting, 'Your disobedience might have brought us all into jeopardy.'[14] Sir Colin's hot blood, so typical of other Scottish nobles at the time, appeared to do the family no lasting harm, for they steadily extended their possessions until his great-grandson, Sir Duncan, was given the title Argyll, in recognition of the family's prominence there.

In 1424, when Sir Duncan featured on the list of eminent hostages offered for the release of King James I from the English, his family's prosperity was illustrated by his annual income of 1500 marks, larger than that of any other hostage except William, heir of Lord Dalkeith, which was set at the same level. Subsequently Sir Duncan was made justiciary and lieutenant within the shire of Argyll. His successor Colin, second Lord Campbell, whom James II created Earl of Argyll in 1457, acquired much additional land for the family by his marriage to Isabel Stewart, one of three daughters of John Lorn of Lorn. Argyll acted as a royal commissioner for James III, negotiating a truce with Edward IV of England in 1463 and another twenty-one years later, when Lord High Chancellor of Scotland, helping to renew the ancient league with France.

When James III's son, the Prince of Rothesay, and others rebelled against the king in 1488 the canny Argyll, among others, obtained a safe conduct from Henry VII to enter England, and he was there at the time of King James' murder, returning after James IV became king of Scotland. Colin's successor Archibald, 2nd earl of Argyll, became Lord High Chancellor obtaining, in typical Campbell fashion, substantial additional (land) charters under the great seal from 1494–1512.[15] In 1504, together with another great Highland magnate, the Earl of Huntly, he was given the king's ultimate trust to suppress the island chieftains under Donald Dubh. Following this, the lordship of the Isles was shared by Argyll and Huntly, with Argyll supervising the southern isles and their adjacent coast, and Huntly policing the northern region.[16] They were so efficient in their duties that from this time until after the battle of Flodden, no serious disturbances occurred in the Western Isles.

Adam Hepburn, 2nd earl of Bothwell

Bothwell was commander of the Scottish rearguard, the third formation beyond the king's personal supervision. His family name originated from their lands in Hebborne, or Hayborne, in Northumberland, and their fighting pedigree was that of a typical border family. Sir Patrick Hepburn of Hales and his son distinguished themselves at the battle of Otterburn, apparently preventing the banner of Douglas falling into enemy hands, and the Scottish chronicler, Fordun, called Patrick Hepburn the younger a 'miles magnanimous et athleta bellicosus',[17] although this hardy soldier was killed in 1402 while making an incursion into England. The Hepburns, like other prominent families, helped to free their king, James I, from English captivity by standing as hostages upon his release. Sir Patrick Hepburn of Hales subsequently became renowned as the conservator of truces conducted with the English in 1449, 1451, 1453, 1457 and 1459, and both his and his family's advancement were marked when, in 1456, he was created a peer under the title of Lord Hales. In 1488 Hales led the Hepburns against James III at Sauchieburn, as a result of which James IV loaded him with favours, creating him Earl of Bothwell and personally girding him with a sword.[18] Bothwell became an intimate of the king, gambling and hawking with him, and in 1492 James IV sent him to negotiate an alliance with France, marking the family's greatest honour so far. When Adam Hepburn, as 2nd earl, succeeded his father the family remained extremely close to the king.

Having judged it necessary to give all his most prominent nobles command roles, in spite of their general ignorance about the art of continental warfare, James might have paused before committing his army to a major battle against Surrey at Flodden, particularly when he had no imperative need nor strong national interests in doing so.

In any case, Scotland's greatest commanders, such as Bruce and Montrose, knew that command must be singular and only when personal dash is needed to give the momentum to assure victory, or when making a last stand, should true leadership take the leader into the forefront of the line. But that was where James quickly took himself, having made no other arrangements for controlling and directing the battle. He naturally commanded the king's division, but he so placed himself that he could not fully comprehend what was happening to the other units within it. As far as the other divisions in his army were concerned, the desirability of controlling and directing them does not seem to have occurred to him.

He never appointed a second-in-command, perhaps fearing the difficulty of choosing from his magnates, always jealous of each other. If this was so, it was another instance of his military shortcomings, for no true commander would have attached more importance to not offending the great families by preferring one of them to the others, than to the inevitable consequences of not doing so. By brushing aside this difficulty he made effective control of his forces impossible. What was worse, he invited chaos by appointing certain of his nobles to joint command; a system that had been adopted earlier by the English at Bannockburn with disastrous results. Bothwell, of the Hepburn family, given sole command of the reserve, provides a crowning illustration of its advantages. Seeing how hard-pressed James was he brought the reserve up with great spirit, forcing his way through towards the king, if not, as he hoped, to save him, at least to die there with his monarch.

As the appalling butcher's bill at Flodden shows, both the Scots' leaders and their followers fought with all their accustomed bravery, although the army was by no means fully united. Amazingly some, such as the Cunninghams and the Montgomeries from Ayrshire, were at feud with each other and their common hatred of the English and loyalty to their king did not serve to alter matters. When, as the battle unfolded, dissensions surfaced among the leaders these were exacerbated by the king's lack of overall control.

It was James IV's misfortune to be fighting just prior to the time in the mid-sixteenth century when wars in Europe would no longer be left to nobles who commanded levies about whom they knew little or for whom they often had the greatest contempt. It was becoming a specialised profession. Men were now speaking and writing of the profession of arms in which professional commanders commanded well-trained soldiers as, for instance, the mercenary Swiss pikemen or the famed Spanish troops. Outstanding generals were acquiring international fame – men such as the Flemish Lamoral, Count of Egmont (1522–68) or the Italian Alessandria Farnese, Duke of Palma (1545–1592). There were still royal commanders such as Gustavus Adolphus of Sweden, the so-called Lion of the North, who was not only an inspired leader but a great champion of the military revolution then taking place, who was followed by the half-mad Charles XII of Sweden for whom the love of fighting seems to have been the driving passion of his life. It is noteworthy, however, that for all his military skill and personal bravery Gustavus relied heavily on his supporting commanders among whom were the Scottish mercenaries, Alexander Leslie, first earl of Leven and Sir John Hepburn.

During his preparations for Flodden James had little opportunity to bring back any prominent Scottish mercenaries to Scotland, whereupon he could have made one his commanding general, and avoided the difficulties of command and control that beset the Scots there. It is doubtful whether he ever considered the possibility for he fancied himself in such a role but, in any case, the outstanding candidate, Bernard Stewart, Signeur d'Aubigny, 'grand chevalier sans reproche', who had excelled himself during the Italian wars, had died soon after his arrival in Scotland five years before. Such an appointment could have at least ensured coherence in the army's command structure which, in such a general's absence, was patently lacking. In fact, James' decision to accept the expertise of French trainers in using the longer continental lances and to place the bulk of his forces in continental style pike columns increased the divisions within his army both by arousing the opposition of his Scottish commanders and by forcing some of his troops to adopt formations quite alien to their fighting traditions.

The problems of James' 'politically correct' command structure can be seen from his order of battle. The royal division was at the centre of the line. To its extreme left the vanguard was made up of both Borderers and Highlanders and jointly commanded by Alexander, Lord Home and Alexander Gordon, earl of Huntly. They were the proud, not to say arrogant, representatives of two different and rival military traditions. The measure of their agreement was liable to be reminiscent of two sulking cats and although Huntly was probably the more able commander, because of his fewer followers he would have had to defer to Home over decisions affecting the full vanguard. To the immediate left of the royal division was another large formation which was to be given the vital task of following up the vanguard in throwing the English forces into headlong retreat. It had three joint commanders, the two veterans, William Hay, earl of Errol, and David Lindsay, earl of Crawford, along with William Graham, earl of Montrose. In his defence, due to his much superior artillery, James IV did not expect to take undue casualties but, whereas the military advantages of its triple command structure elude immediate understanding, it enabled James – at one fell swoop – to satisfy three of his insatiable old military families.

Another instance of joint command came with James' division of Highlanders stationed in their traditional place to the right of the battle line. They were commanded by their two leading representatives, Archibald Campbell, earl of Argyll and Matthew Stewart, earl of Lennox, who had famously been on opposite sides against James IV in the late fifteenth century. The prospect of swift and concerted decision-making in this formation, therefore, seemed slim.

Apart from such flawed command arrangements James aroused expectations about inflicting a crushing blow on the English when most of his forces were committed for a short engagement only, and any pursuit into England could not be contemplated. James had already proved himself an outstanding Scottish king but at Flodden he was out of his depth; a true statesman would not have fought there and a natural warrior would not have fought there as he did.

PART THREE

Face to Face

CHAPTER SEVEN

≈

OPENING MOVES

Climate is what you expect but weather is what you get
Anonymous

HOSTILITIES BETWEEN ENGLAND and Scotland had in
fact opened a fortnight before James IV's army left
Edinburgh's Burghmuir. On 5 August 1513, a Scottish raiding
party some 7000 strong, mounted on their tough, wiry ponies,
crossed into English Northumberland. They were led by the
border chieftain Lord Home. With many of the watch towers
still derelict after James IV's foray of 1496–7, the raiders were
able to burn farms and villages almost at will, taking items of
value and driving off large numbers of cattle before setting
fire to the dwellings.

Although still far away in Pontefract Castle, the English
commander, Surrey, had received reports of impending trouble,
with tales of the Scots removing their cattle and other possessions northwards. He accordingly despatched the Yorkshire
commander, Sir William Bulmer, with 200 mounted archers,
authorising him to monitor the situation and then act as he
thought fit. Bulmer called out some 'gentlemen of the north'[1]
and having gathered about 1000 men he decided to ambush
the returning raiders when encumbered with their booty. On
the small plain of Milfield, just north of Wooler, the English
concealed themselves among clumps of yellow broom which
commonly grew there to the height of men's shoulders. The
raiders fell into the trap: a cloud of well-directed arrows killed
500–600 of them but the others, although heavily impeded,
were said to have fought like men before making their escape
to the border. Most of the booty fell into the attackers' hands
and, although the Scottish leader escaped he left his Home

banner with the English.[2] Small as it was, the clash was a bad start for Scottish arms and they acknowledged this by naming it the 'Ill raid'.

In the meanwhile, the two countries' main forces were assembling and preparing to approach each other. Although information about the Scottish army is incomplete it is known that on 19 August, following the firing of a signal gun and the command 'Forward', the units that had assembled on Edinburgh's Burghmuir stepped off upon their historic journey. Rain made the roads soft but they were soon through Dalkeith and across rolling country before climbing the edge of the Lammermuir hills on the their way to the second muster point at Ellem Kirk. Here they joined units from the east before the whole army marched more than twenty miles to Coldstream on the Tweed where, on 22 August, they probably forded the river close to its junction with its tributary, the Till. Advancing up the Tweed's south bank they made camp at Twizelhaugh, about three miles from the great English castle of Norham. The speed of the Scottish advance was remarkable and demonstrates how many lessons about moving the cumbrous guns had been learned from the 1497 campaign. Such rapid movement was important, for it gave James a range of offensive options before English levies could be moved into the area, although it meant there had been little or no opportunity to re-order his units at Ellem, or to rehearse them in the new tactics taught by their French instructors.

However, at least one commentator has drawn attention to what he saw as the Scottish nobles' anticipation of approaching death, when, on 24 August, while the army was still at Twizelhaugh, they requested their king to pass an ordinance exempting any who died of wounds or disease from the payment of fees 'of wardship, relief or marriage'.[3] In fact it was a normal concession before major battles – it had been granted by Bruce before Bannockburn – and it probably said more about James' military inexperience in not pre-empting the request than any presentiments among

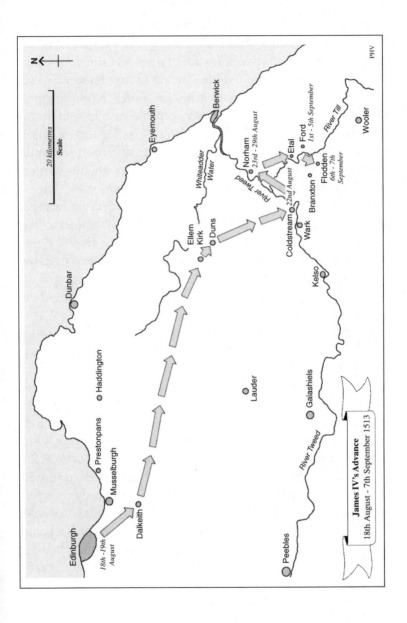

Scale
20 kilometres

N

PHV

Edinburgh
18th - 19th August
Prestonpans
Musselburgh
Dalkeith
Haddington
Dunbar
Eyemouth
Berwick
Ellem
Kirk
Duns
Whiteadder Water
Norham
23rd - 29th August
Etal
Ford
1st - 5th September
River Till
Wooler
River Tweed
22nd August
Coldstream
Wark
Branxton
Flodden
6th - 7th September
Lauder
Kelso
Galashiels
River Tweed
Peebles

James IV's Advance
18th August - 7th September 1513

men who were still unaware of the king's plans. In fact, the Scottish king's initial objectives were in line with those of his 1497 campaign and indeed his first target was the very castle that had thwarted him earlier. Strong as its defences were, Norham could not compare with the much larger fortress of Berwick-on-Tweed, which was capable of withstanding a lengthy siege during which time English relief forces would be virtually certain to arrive. Norham was different, for while undoubtedly tough and in a pivotal position on the border, it had no seaward communications and, in any case, James' gunners were likely to have registered its vulnerable features in 1497. Built largely in the twelfth century, the simple box-like construction of its massive tower overlooking the river was not to its advantage. Eighteen feet thick in places, it lacked bastions for carrying counter-artillery and could not be expected to withstand concentrated fire from massive guns launching their 60lb missiles.[4]

As with the 'Ill raid', Surrey had already done what he could to counter the expected Scottish attacks. He ensured that Berwick's fortifications were in readiness and he had written to John Ainslow, the constable of Norham Castle, to inquire about his state of defence, assuring the constable that, if attacked, as in 1497, he would come to his relief. Ainslow replied with remarkable confidence, 'praying God that the King of Scots would come with his puissance for he would defend the castle until King Henry VIII returned from France to raise the siege.'[5] Ainslow had already received additional quantities of ammunition and his confidence would have been further bolstered by the castle's record against previous Scottish attacks. Although it had been taken in 1138, 1136, and 1322, the Scots had failed in 1215, 1318, 1319, 1327 and, of course, in 1497.

This time it would be different. James' heaviest guns were not likely to have crossed the Tweed with the rest of the Scottish army but to have been dragged along its northern bank and positioned near James IV's church at Ladykirk,[6] to pound the castle from short range. One can visualise the steady fire of the huge guns, probably three operating together with their crews protected by wooden screens or mantlets, equipped with doors that could be opened immediately before firing and then reclosed during the reloading. Most missiles would be aimed directly at the castle's walls, although when elevated they could deliver plunging fire into its heart. The heavy shots would shake the walls as they crashed against them, eventually dislodging stones and causing gaps and cracks to appear. Under the bombardment those facing the cannon became seriously depleted and the north-east corner of the great tower was shattered. For six days the pounding went on and on three successive days the Scottish king launched costly attacks, but his troops were largely inexperienced in siege operations and they failed to break in, for the constable and his garrison conducted an energetic and spirited defence. The actual size of the garrison is not known but in 1523, for instance, it numbered 20 gunners, 70 archers and 100 horsemen.[7] Even when supplemented for the anticipated attack it was unlikely to have exceeded 300 men. Although the damage was serious the defenders remained defiant, retaining control of the keep and the inner bailey walls.

However, by 29 August, Ainslow had exhausted his ammunition and he knew that, if he continued to hold out, both he and his garrison would run the risk of execution. He therefore surrendered, giving James and his artillery a notable success: in one week the combination of heavy guns and infantry assaults had brought the result that had eluded him in 1497, despite a siege lasting six times as long. Following his victory the Scottish king gave the castle over to his soldiers who plundered its accumulated stock of food and wine, together with its rich furnishings.[8]

With no English force to contend with, James advanced slowly southwards down the right-hand side of the River Till. In the process he took the castles of Wark and Etal, both in a state of decay from earlier Scottish raids, and then went on to Ford Castle, a further three miles south. Responsibility for its defence lay in the hands of Lady Elizabeth Heron in the absence of her husband, William, who was being held prisoner in Scotland as a hostage for the bastard John Heron who (as mentioned before) had, in 1508, murdered the Scottish warden of the middle March, Sir Robert Ker of Ferniehurst, on a border truce day. In fact the English had pardoned John Heron a fortnight earlier, but he had not yet returned. The Scots demanded its surrender from Lady Heron, who complied with their request on or about 1 September.[9] James thereupon made Ford Castle his headquarters, remaining there until 5 September while his troops fanned out across the surrounding region, destroying any remaining peel towers and plundering as they went.

Reports of James IV's own activities at this time have varied. The Scottish writers Pitscottie and Buchanan, followed by the eighteenth-century English writer George Ridpath, attributed his delay at Ford Castle to his falling under the spell of Lady Heron, a beautiful woman, with his son Alexander Stewart, archbishop of St Andrews, simultaneously succumbing to Lady Heron's daughter. This is rather too neat an explanation, particularly as the two Scottish writers were alone among the near contemporary chroniclers in putting this forward as a contributory factor to the outcome at Flodden. While James IV did agree to spare Ford Castle, it was on condition Lady Heron handed over Lord Johnstone and Alexander Home, who was being held in England following their capture during the 'Ill raid'.[10] She failed to do so and the castle was burned down.

No English report on James' activities prior to Flodden and his delay at Ford Castle made any mention of Pitscottie's charge of 'stinking adultery and fornication'. James undoubtedly had other problems without allowing himself to be so seduced, including the wear and tear sustained by both his weapons and men. The intensive use of the artillery at Norham compelled him to send to Edinburgh for draught oxen, fresh

1. James IV by an unknown artist. (Private collection; reproduced by permission of The National Galleries of Scotland)

2. Margaret Tudor Queen of Scotland, by Daniel Mytens. (From the Royal Collection of Her Majesty Queen Elizabeth II)

3. Henry VIII by Gerard Horebout. (Private collection; reproduced by permission of The National Galleries of Scotland)

THO.ˢ HOWARD EARL OF SURRY
after Duke of Norfolk

The Autograph of Tho. Earl of Surry

4. Thomas Howard, 2nd Duke of Norfolk and Earl of Surrey by an unknown artist. (Private collection; reproduced by permission of The National Galleries of Scotland)

5. Branxton Church. (Photograph by Barbara Reese)

6. Scottish pike and English bill. (Illustration by Paul Vickers)

7 & 8. Scottish 36 pounder cannon. (Illustrations by Paul Vickers)

9 & 10. English 2 pounder falcon. (Illustrations by Paul Vickers)

11. The Flodden Memorial. (Photograph by Paul Vickers)

ammunition and new wheels for the gun carriages.[11] The problems experienced by his ordinary soldiers were more important still. From the commencement of his siege at Norham the weather had been bad, cold, with high winds and rain, 'No scarce one hour of fair weather all the time the Scots army had lain within England.' Under such conditions his army's strength was steadily diminishing. There were difficulties in feeding such a massive number, for little was found in the bleak and stripped regions of Northumberland, and in particular the contingents who had travelled long distances before coming to muster were bound to be running short of provisions. Inevitably, some of their representatives would have been sent home to bring back fresh supplies.

James' battle rolls were also diminished by the casualties suffered during the Norham siege and even more by the far larger numbers that had set off for home with their plunder from both Norham and other buildings in the Till valley. For them the campaign was over. In addition a number of men were falling sick. Pestilence had been present since the muster but it became more serious in the adverse weather. Whatever the reasons, some straggling started very early, for on 5 September there were comments during an Edinburgh council meeting about soldiers who had already left the army and re-entered the city with their plunder.[12] Such losses, however, should not be given disproportionate importance. The army was not haemorrhaging men: after Ford, James still had a force of more than 30,000, which was large by Scottish standards, undoubtedly well-equipped and bigger than anything Surrey could assemble at short notice. Any desertions served to eliminate the weaker elements and pare it down to those most likely to perform well.

Notwithstanding, such difficulties denied the Scottish king his most ambitious and unlikely option, namely of advancing deep into England and threatening its heartland. James' dubious boast of being in York by Michaelmas[13] was now quite beyond him and, in any case, Surrey's forces barred his way.

It is doubtful, however, if he ever seriously intended to take such a risk with what was essentially a feudal army. Whatever James' own inclination for battlefield success, his strategic aim seemed best achieved by assembling an impressive army and by pitting it stylishly against the English border defences, thus raising the possibility of further invasion and persuading the English to draw back part, or even the bulk, of their army from France. A further advantage of this policy was that, by the time the English could react and send troops from France or even others from middle or northern England, they would be too late in the campaigning year to prevent the Scots from moving back across the border.

The success or otherwise of James' plans, of course, hinged upon the ability and responses of his opponent. Facing him the seventy-year-old Earl of Surrey, Commander of the North, had the task of alerting the northern English levies, assembling them into effective formations and moving them up to the border. Notwithstanding his age, Surrey's energy and determination were evident and he was assisted by the efficient defence arrangements instigated by the Tudors. From 30 June, the day on which Henry VIII sailed from France and before the Scots showed definite signs of attacking, Surrey began his counter preparations. By 12 July stocks of grain had been sent by sea to Newcastle and he was collecting his 500-strong retinue of experienced soldiers. Surrey also arranged for his artillery to be despatched from London to Durham.

Accompanied by his large retinue he then set off for the north; reaching Hull on 22 July and Pontefract by the end of the month. From Pontefract Surrey issued a summons to discover the numbers of men capable of being raised from across the north of England and to give their commanders a warning order for subsequent mobilisation. Messages were sent to all 'Lordes Spirituall, Temporall, Knyghtes, Gentilmenne or other who had tenaunts or were rulers of townes or liberties [able to make men] to certify what numbers of able men horsed and harnessed, they were able to make within houres warnynge

and to give there attendaunce.'[14] At the same time he called
on the co-operation of the fleet that had completed its task
of escorting the English army across the Channel and he
alerted his son, the Lord Admiral, to stand ready to join him
together with another contingent of experienced soldiers and
sailors. When, on 25 August, Surrey learned that the Scots
had crossed the Tweed he sent out a predetermined signal
calling the levies to arms and on the following day moved from
Pontefract to York. That night, using the powers given him,
he ordered York's Lord Mayor to call out the city's trained
bands, and made arrangements for a war purse of £10,800 to
be collected from the north's unofficial paymaster, the abbot
of St Mary's.[15]

Like the Scots, the English movements were much affected
by the weather and after leaving York, Surrey experienced 'the
foulest day and night that could be' when his guide was almost
drowned in front of him, before reaching Durham on the 29th.
There he learned of the rapid fall of Norham Castle: the Scots
had shown their teeth. After hearing mass in the cathedral,
Surrey asked to borrow the famous banner of St Cuthbert,
which had proved so inspirational in the English victory of
1138. That evening wind and rain beat against his lodgings
but, undeterred, on the next day the old earl, with his party
further augmented by contingents from Durham, set out for
Newcastle which the mud-splattered party reached before
darkness. There his pre-planning bore fruit, for he was met
by Lord Dacre and other northern gentlemen, including Sir
William Bulmer and Sir Marmaduke Constable, together with
his artillery train. Dacre had already demonstrated his own
commitment against the attackers with a letter to the bishop
of Durham in which he proposed to 'overdrive the time' to
make invasion harder for the Scots.[16] That night was even
wilder than the previous one, the 'wind blew curragiously' and
Surrey was very fearful for his son, the Lord Admiral, in case
he 'should perish that night upon the sea'.[17]

Over the next four days the waterlogged tracks around

Newcastle filled with men, both mounted and on foot, struggling to join the muster. Some came from Lancashire, from places like Hornby and Lancaster, and many Yorkshiremen from Wensleydale and Swaledale, from the North Riding and the towns of Skipton and Hull, to join those from the city of York who were already with Surrey. The latter were led by their official swordbearer bearing the city's semi-royal banner of a red cross and five golden lions. Surrey welcomed them all as they reported in, but there was still no sign of his son.

By 3 September Surrey felt he could wait no longer; the contingents presently scattered throughout Newcastle and its surrounding countryside had to be brought under firm leadership. He ordered them to march north and muster on a small flat plain close to the village of Bolton-in-Glendale near Alnwick, about twenty miles away from the Scottish army. On the 4th Surrey was finally joined by his son and 1100 experienced fighting men, including much-needed officers and twelve professional German gunners from Danzig, to assist with the artillery. Unsurprisingly, the Lord Admiral's safe arrival delighted his father for he was considered to be a good commander, 'very wise, hardy and of great credence and experience'[18] and furthermore he gave Surrey someone of his own kin who possessed both the energy and will to carry out his orders. At Bolton Surrey raised the royal standard and the banner of St George before placing his army into its composite units. Overall it was split into two main divisions, a vanguard and a rather smaller rearguard. He appointed the Lord Admiral as his vanguard commander, retaining command of the rearguard himself. The following table shows how both main divisions were sub-divided into a centre formation and two wings.

Apart from Surrey's and the Admiral's professionals, eighty per cent or more of the English army were indentured retainers. Geographically, Lancashire and Cheshire provided up to 9000 men (the vast majority of whom were retainers of the Stanleys); a further 9000 came from Yorkshire, with Durham,

English Vanguard
Commander: Thomas Howard, the Lord Admiral

Left Wing
Commander: Sir Marmaduke Constable
With 2000 men
A family unit under captains that included his brother, three sons, two cousins and a son-in-law, Sir William Percy, who brought his retainers from Northumberland. 1000 Lancashire men were posted to this wing to raise its complement.

Centre
Directly Under the Admiral's command
This totalled 9000 men: 1000 were soldiers from the fleet, dressed in Surrey's livery of green and white and led by fifteen Captains of Ships; 2000 were the Bishop of Durham's retainers protecting the sacred banner of St Cuthbert and commanded by Sir William Bulmer and Lord Lumley. With the latter were contingents from Northumberland and Durham. The majority of this division, however, came from Yorkshire, including Lord Clifford's followers from the Pennine Dale wearing red wyverns on their jackets and Lord Conyers with men from the North Riding with many lesser knights and gentlemen.

Right Wing
Commander Edmund Howard
(the Admiral's younger brother)
With 3000 men. 1000 were from Cheshire, including those from Macclesfield and 300 tenants of the Abbey of the Vale Royal. 500 men came from Lancashire with the remainder from Yorkshire, including Hull's town levy and a Doncaster contingent, along with 200 of the Admiral's men, under Captain Maurice Berkeley of the *Mary George*.

English Rearguard
Commander: The Earl of Surrey

Left Wing
Commander: Sir Edward Stanley
Probably about 3500 men strong. All Stanley tenants from Lancashire and Cheshire with the family's senior retainers acting as their captains.

Centre
Under Surrey's command
About 5000 men. This included Surrey's retinue and headquarters staff of 500 men. Surrey's division was composed almost completely of Yorkshiremen: south Yorkshiremen under George Darcy; Swaledale and Wensleydale men under Lord Scrope of Bolton, citizens of York, tenants of the abbot of Whitby and some East Riding men under their archdeacon.

Right Wing
Commander Lord Dacre
Less than 3500 men. Dacre had his own followers, 'border prickers' from Cumberland and Westmoreland, along with a Northumberland troop under the Bastard Heron totalling about 1500 men. Surrey therefore allocated other horsemen from Bamboroughshire and Tynemouth and 1800 Lancashire retainers of James Stanley, Bishop of Ely, commanded by his bastard son, John. These had the eagle claw badges and three gold crowns on their coats and fought under the banner of St Audrey.

Northumberland, Cumberland and Westmoreland providing the rest.

While the rank and file were being allocated officers and sergeants, the English high command spent the greater part of 4 September considering the strategic and tactical options open to them. By assembling such a considerable army at short notice they had effectively checked a wholesale Scottish invasion and spared the border counties from widespread pillage. But what now? Lord Dacre raised the dangerous possibility of the Scots moving back into Scotland and waiting there until the adverse weather and a long supply line forced the English to disband, upon which the Scots might resume a southwards offensive. Because of the nature of the Scottish feudal army, in which most of its men were on strictly short service this was rightly thought to be no more than a slim possibility. After much discussion it was agreed that while their soldiers were well fed and relatively fresh they should try to bring the Scots to battle before 9 September when their full rations were expected to run out. Such a strategy posed major risks but, even if it were not successful, the Scots would not be expected to escape unscathed; there was also the safety net of additional levies being available in England together with the further possibility of units returning from France.

If they meant to fight, both James IV and Surrey could cite good reasons for doing so. Prior to this they could expect to exchange the formal threats and counter-threats usually preceding a major conflict at this time and, even more important, to manoeuvre their forces in order to gain positional advantage.

≈

CHAPTER EIGHT

JOCKEYING FOR POSITION

'Let us list and march I say
Over the hills and far away!'
English army song

ONCE SURREY HAD decided to fight he sent the customary herald to James IV carrying the English proposal with regard to a possible time and place for the battle. This proved, however, to be far more than an habitual and chivalrous gesture, for the two letters carried by his herald, Rouge Croix Pursuivant, were expressly designed to goad the Scottish king into battle, rather than allow him the option of moving back to Scotland. On 5 September Surrey sent Rouge Croix to Ford Castle, where he believed the Scottish headquarters to be, with two provocative messages.

The first, from Surrey himself, accused James IV that 'contrary to his oath and league and unnaturally against all reason and conscience [he] had invaded his brother's realm of England ... burning, spoiling and destroying and cruelly murdering the English king's subjects.'[1] It concluded with Surrey's formal challenge, namely that he was ready to do battle up to 9 September. Surrey's accusatory letter, together with his formal offer of battle, was accompanied by another, even more inflammatory and threatening. This came from Surrey's son, the Lord Admiral, who wrote scornfully that James IV's much prized navy had not been able to stand against his English ships but had fled to France via the coast of Ireland. Thomas Howard reminded the Scottish king that he, the Admiral, had been responsible for the death of Sir Andrew Barton, James' revered sea-captain, and he followed this with the ugly and distinctly non-chivalric prediction that in the event of a battle, 'He nor none of hys compargnye shoulde take no Scottishe noblemen prysoner ... unless it were the Kynge's awne person for he sayde he trusted to none other curtesye at the handes of the Scottes.'[2]

The other traditional function of heralds at this time was to give their commanders as much information as they could regarding their opponents' forces and dispositions. James therefore seized Rouge Croix to prevent the English from knowing he had moved his army from the neighbourhood of Ford Castle across the River Till to take up a strong position on Flodden Hill. The Scottish reply was carried by James' own herald, Islay, whom the English in their turn then kept prisoner until Rouge Croix's safe return.

The Scottish king had no intention of making things easy for Surrey and his herald did not approach the English camp until midnight of 5 September. However, the message he carried, that the Scots would wait for Surrey until noon of Friday 9 September,[3] no doubt delighted them. In response, during the next day the English moved forward, in combat order, to the village of Wooler and onwards to Wooler Haugh nearby, where, from the left bank of the Till, Surrey could look upon the small, flat plain of Milfield (famous for the earlier clash during the 'ill raid'). Because it was such 'a convenyent and fair grounde' he expected the Scots would make their own approach to it on the morning of the 7th.

In fact, when the Scots released Rouge Croix and returned him to Surrey on the 7th, he brought bad news. The Scottish army had decided to wait on Flodden Hill, a feature like a fortress 'enclosed with three great mountaynes, soe that there was noe passage nor entre unto hym but oon waye wher was laied marvelous and great ordenance of gunnes.'[4] Flodden mass, a lower outlier of the Cheviots, was in 1513 a bare saddle-backed hill over 500 feet above sea level, well capable of daunting any would-be attacker. Here the Scots army made their camp on its north-eastern slopes. To the east it sloped very steeply, while to the west any approach was protected by a large belt of marshy ground, with the Moneylaws and Branxton hills to the north. The obvious approach was from the south, up long and relatively even slopes, but the Scottish artillery effectively covered this route.

After agreeing to fight, James' decision to occupy such a position was probably taken on the counsel of his French military advisers for, during the early sixteenth century, entrenched camps had featured regularly in European campaigns. By occupying Flodden Hill James was certainly not acting in the traditions of Wallace and Bruce.[5] While both undoubtedly made shrewd use of the battlefield opportunities offered them by Scotland's natural features, if they had wanted to tempt the English into attacking them they would never have placed a larger army (a luxury which, in any case, they never enjoyed) with superior firepower astride a near impregnable feature. At Stirling Bridge Wallace had a much weaker army than his opponent and, while Stirling's narrow river bridge slowed the English build-up until he could gauge when to attack them, the English were at least crossing over onto flat carse-land which offered a chance of success for both sides. A year later Wallace chose an unimpressive hill near Falkirk – the site of an old Roman mile-castle – relying on his new tactical formation to blunt the attack of a superior English army. And at Bannockburn, where Bruce gained the greatest of all Scottish victories over the 'auld enemy', the English themselves chose the dangerous and confined area for their camp that persuaded Bruce to attack them with his much smaller army.

James' decision to occupy Flodden Hill raises the question of whether he genuinely wanted to fight at all. He was, of course, not compelled to and there were perfectly good reasons for staying there and placing the onus of a disadvantageous attack on the English. In this way, he would undoubtedly have kept his agreement with France without taking undue risks. Although James was yet to know it, on whatever terms he decided to fight England's northern levies, he had not drawn off any measurable part of the English army from France.

Indeed on the very day he crossed the Tweed, Therouanne had capitulated and Henry VIII's siege artillery was preparing to bombard the second and greater prize of Tournai.

In his favour James had destroyed Norham Castle and other English border defences, he had compelled the English northern levies to mobilise and caused 1100 soldiers and sailors, together with the Lord Admiral, to return from the continent, although the latter had at no time been part of Henry's front line formations. How much further should a Scottish king go for France? With a fragile supply line, steadily falling rolls and the majority of his men committed for a maximum of forty days' service only, James lacked the capability to mount a telling invasion of northern England. The decision, therefore, to camp on an impregnable hill rather than hazard everything on what now seemed a strategically pointless engagement, seemed sound policy.

James' occupation of Flodden Hill undoubtedly presented Surrey with a fearsome problem. His herald's reports on the strength of the Scottish position would have become common knowledge among his troops and the muffled, but powerful, reverberations coming from the direction of Flodden, as the Scottish artillery adjusted their ranges and lines of fire, would have served to confirm it. English morale would not have been raised by the news that wagons from Newcastle carrying much-needed food and beer had been intercepted and taken by English border raiders.

Surrey called another council of war. This rapidly concluded that a direct attack on Flodden was not a practical option but, although food shortages appeared to limit their offensive options, the council agreed they must try to prevent James from slipping back across the border. In the first instance, they decided to try and bring the Scottish king off his massif by challenging his sense of honour. A no doubt nervous Rouge Croix returned to Flodden at five in the afternoon with a letter signed by all eighteen members of the military council reproving James for following up his offer to fight by occupying his fortress-like position. It asked him to come down to Milfield to give battle some time between twelve noon and three p.m. of the following day (8 September).[6]

The herald was also told that in the event of James' refusal he had the council's authority to tell the Scottish king that Surrey 'would look for no more of his delays'; he was saved from this dangerous duty when James refused to see him and one of the Scottish King's gentlemen both took the letter and returned with the following uncompromising reply. 'Show to the Earl of Surrey that it beseemeth him not, being an Earl, so largely to attempt a great prince. His grace will take and hold his ground at his own pleasure and not at the assigning of the Earl of Surrey.'[7] Whether the king's rage was real or not – and his quickness to take offence and well-known pride make it likely to have been real – Surrey decided that by staying on Flodden Hill James had not acted chivalrously and had, in fact, not met his challenge. This therefore left the English commander free to attack the Scots – which had always been his intention – where he could best bring it about.

However much Surrey might have felt frustrated by James' tactics, any other commander of the northern levies would have been satisfied with the outcome. He had faithfully carried out his sovereign's instructions and, by his rapid mobilisation and move northwards, had not only checked the Scots' invasion but faced them down over a possible battle. If more food could be brought from Berwick, for instance, the army could maintain its vigilance until the Scottish feudal array would itself be forced to move away to the north. But for Surrey and his eldest son, resentful at being excluded from the French campaign, this was not enough: out of favour as they were, the campaign offered them their best, and possibly last, chance of additional renown. It is also possible Surrey might have been encouraged to take further initiatives by the occasion, ten years before, when he escorted Princess Margaret to Edinburgh for her wedding and had got onto familiar terms with the Scottish king. He would have learned of James' chivalric attitude to warfare and might possibly have considered ways of exploiting it.

For whatever reasons, in contrast to James' safety first policy Surrey was about to take an enormous gamble. At midday on 8 September, soon after receiving James' reply, he ordered his army, including his twenty-two guns, to strike camp and prepare to move north. Just beyond Milfield they crossed to the Till's eastern bank, thus giving themselves some protection from the Scots on Flodden Hill, some three miles away. After walking the ground in unsettled weather the author is sure the Scots on Flodden would, in fact, have had the utmost difficulty in keeping track of the extended English column. The English had two possible routes towards their northerly objective of Bar moor. Using the more westerly one – much the likeliest to be chosen – they would certainly have been difficult to detect, while the parallel but somewhat longer one further east would have been almost completely screened from Flodden.

In the Scottish camp there appeared to be different reactions to the English move. The majority thought they would continue northwards and, possibly after retaking Norham Castle, go on to attack the Scottish border regions. Such a possibility was bound to make James' commanders nervous, especially those with border estates, and some opted for a return to Scotland. Their discussions appeared to have been hampered by a lack of firm information since few – or no – scouts had been sent out to track the English. At this time the Scots seemed to have contented themselves with strengthening their position by burning small villages, such as Fisher's Steads, lying on the rim of the wet ground covering their eastern flank nearest the English.

In fact, Surrey's plan was to improve his tactical position by either persuading the Scots to come off Flodden Hill by threatening their line of retreat,[8] or to put himself in a position to move on them from the rear. By that evening the English army completed its long march of more than sixteen miles to Bar moor, where the 500-foot Watchlaw Hill to

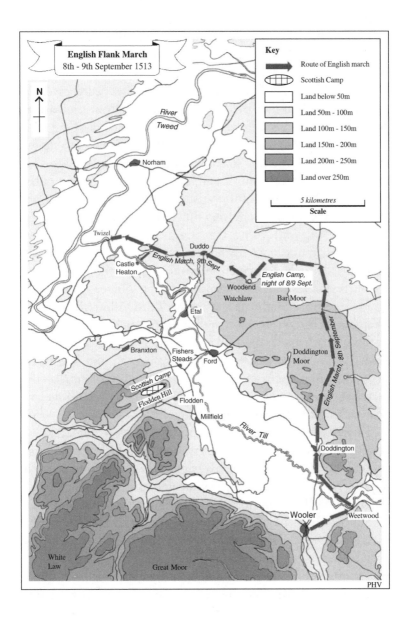

Key

Route of English march

Scottish Camp

Land below 50m

Land 50m - 100m

Land 100m - 150m

Land 150m - 200m

Land 200m - 250m

Land over 250m

5 kilometres

Scale

English Flank March
8th - 9th September 1513

N

River Tweed

Norham

Twizel

Duddo

Castle Heaton

English March, 9th Sept.

English Camp, night of 8/9 Sept.

Woodend

Watchlaw

Bar Moor

Etal

Branxton

Fishers Steads

Ford

Doddington Moor

English March, 8th September

Scottish Camp

Flodden Hill

Flodden

Millfield

River Till

Doddington

Wooler

Weetwood

White Law

Great Moor

PHV

its immediate west protected them from 'the danger of gun shot'. Despite inevitable fears, they had not been raked by the powerful Scottish guns from Flodden which, even when set at full elevation, lacked sufficient range.

For such a hazardous journey local guides were essential and it is probable that the English benefited from the bastard John Heron and his followers' intimate knowledge of the area. As the weary and hungry men set up camp and attempted to make fires with the soaking wood available, we are told 'they much cold did suffer'[9] and, doubtless complaining in the way of soldiers, distastefully washed down their short rations with freezing stream water, as they exchanged wagers on the possibility of confronting the Scottish invaders. They knew Surrey would not have taken them so far without good reason and any sense of anticipation would have been heightened by Surrey's messengers summoning their officers to another council of war. Many had seen the Lord Admiral climbing Watchlaw Hill to reconnoitre the Scottish positions and those in his party passed on the news that from its summit 'he perfectly saw [the Scots], discovered them all and had made his plans.' Any decision would be governed no doubt by the fact that, search as he would, he could find no practicable way of attacking Flodden from the flanks.

Those who assembled in Surrey's tent were told that he and the Admiral remained determined to attack the Scottish army. John Heron was then likely to have outlined the possible approaches to the Scots' position and the conformation of Branxton Hill to the north of Flodden, which was not only of almost equal height but separated from Flodden merely by a shallow saddle. Branxton was clearly the key feature for a viable attack; once astride it they would be able to block the Scottish line of communications and move from there to Flodden where they could meet the Scots on relatively equal terms. To achieve this, however, meant another long and arduous approach march. From the north Branxton Hill could be climbed by a series of long but by no means difficult slopes, but prior to this the advancing columns had to keep out of the sight and range of the Scottish guns, and above all they needed to cross the wide and fast-flowing river Till.

With Branxton Hill their objective the Admiral outlined his plans. They were to resume their march northwards but then change direction, moving in a sweep from east to west. At its tip the vanguard, together with the artillery and light cavalry, would cross the River Till by Twizell Bridge, while the rear-guard would attempt to cross the river at a point two kilometres or so to the east. Once across, both formations would close up, remaining in dead ground while they crossed a marshy valley containing the relatively small stream of the Pallinsburn on whose further side lay the lower slopes of Branxton Hill. This approach required a further day's hard marching, not ideal preparation for hungry men who would need all their strength for the anticipated hand-to-hand fighting. Although the Admiral could not be expected to overemphasise it, the plan also needed considerable luck, for the proposal to split the army in order to cross the Till was particularly risky. And once across the second obstacle of the Pallinsburn the English had to ascend the initial slopes of Branxton Hill before tackling the main climb towards the summit from where, by way of a saddle, they could at last come upon their objective, the Scottish army at Flodden, not only superior in numbers and fire power but also well rested. Finally in the event of them being thrown back, the Till would bar their most obvious line of withdrawal. After some discussion all eventually agreed that 'after crossing Twizel Bridge the army would give battle to the Scots on the hill.'[10]

For an army with Surrey as its leader, his eldest son its vanguard commander and another son in a senior command position, there was little chance of the plan being counter-manded nor, under the Howards' tough regime, any doubts about it being followed faithfully. Here the Howards were fortunate, for the army's other influential commanders, such as Lord Dacre, old Sir Marmaduke Constable and even their arch rivals like the Stanleys, were north-country magnates who also viewed the Scots as their traditional rivals and could be relied upon to fight against them enthusiastically.

Surrey's initiatives so far had been outstanding. The English army's move to Bar moor changed both the strategic and tactical balance: it not only threatened James IV's communications and questioned his safe return to Scotland, but gave cover to Berwick, the obvious source of fresh supplies for the English. What might earlier have seemed to the Scots like an impregnable position capable of defeating any attack from the south, had become a trap: not only were the English blocking James' return northwards but, with the obligatory period of service for his feudal levies fast diminishing, any move south would also be exceedingly hazardous. To the south-east Newcastle was much too large a nut to crack, while even Alnwick Castle, only half the distance away, could hold him up for longer than could be afforded. To the south-west the wild and barren Cheviot hills represented a nightmare for any army, and James had little chance of worthwhile supplies and plunder until he reached the towns along the old Roman wall. In the extreme west the great fortress of Carlisle presented too great an obstacle, and even towns like Hexham could be expected to offer determined opposition.

In contrast, from the vicinity of Bar moor Surrey could now call on supplies from nearby Berwick, while further quantities could be sent up from the south by sea. After obtaining supplies indentured troops could stay in the field longer than the Scots who, if they decided to return home, were likely to cross the Tweed at nearby Coldstream. But Surrey was determined to bring the Scots to battle, and by leaving Bar moor and moving west he shut the door even more firmly against James' return home, at the same time offering him a challenge that could not be refused.

After the initial jockeying for advantage the two armies, following their commanders' orders, were now seeking each other's throats. James IV seemed about to be granted his battle, if not the one of his dreams; whereas his guns outmatched the opposition's light artillery the prevailing ground conditions would severely test the ability of his newly-formed pike columns to keep their fighting balance. For Surrey, the odds seemed even higher; he had decided to lead tired men against a superior enemy and, by so doing, had exceeded Henry VIII's remit for defending England's northern boundary. Defeat would bring a certain and terrible penalty for the Howard family, if not at the hands of the Scots then from their own king.

CHAPTER NINE

≈

THE GUNS SPEAK

Both advantage and danger are inherent in manoeuvre
Sun Tzu, *The Art of War*

FOLLOWING SURREY'S COUNCIL of war the subordinate English commanders returned to their own lines and explained to the men their formations' role during the second day of the approach march. By passing on the orders to leave their draught horses, tents and baggage behind no one could doubt the determination of the Howards to seek battle or fail to realise that they were making no arrangements for withdrawal. Apart from those on sentry duty, everyone was ordered to get some rest: the most senior enjoyed the shelter of their tents, but the vast majority remained exposed to the wind and rain and only the lucky ones found billets round the smoky camp fires. Most tried to cat nap under dripping trees or in folds in the ground to the lea of gorse bushes. Whatever sleep they had, for all – great and ordinary soldiers alike – reveille was at 4 o'clock in the morning, ready for the move off one hour later.[1] Their remaining bread or meat would be eaten on the march.

They set out on time and after a full six hours' marching the vanguard, including its toiling gun trains and light cavalry, completed the seven-mile journey to Twizel Bridge, which they began to cross. At about the same time the rearguard, under Surrey, which had turned south about two miles before, followed a winding track to where the Till could be forded and, having worked their way down its steep northern bank, locked arms and crossed the swollen river before struggling up the river's southern bank. The Till was Surrey's Rubicon; once across, his army was set on its final phase before battle. Sound commander that he was, he was certainly no Alexander

nor Henry V, but he nonetheless showed his awareness of
the move's significance by addressing his captains after their
crossing, asking that they fight 'like Englishmen, this day, take
my part like men, which part is the King's part', to which they
jointly responded that they 'would serve the King and him truly
that day'.[2]

With the wind and rain in their faces, both wings of the army
now in battle order resumed their southerly march, for they
had the better part of four more miles to cover before ascend-
ing the Branxton ridge that rose in places to 500 feet. At their
earlier rate this meant a further four hours for the crawling
millipede of hungry men. Three miles on they descended
into the valley adjoining Branxton village, through the base
of which ran the stream of the Pallinsburn (sometimes known
as the Sandy ford) which crossed their front before entering the
Till to the east. It was, of course, far less of an obstacle than the
Till, being 'but a man's step over',[3] but after such unceasing
rain the ground along both banks had became a morass. Here
they benefited from John Heron's local knowledge, for they
were directed to a track that disappeared within trees screening
the burn and crossed it along a low stone causeway. Both the
track and its causeway were undoubtedly narrow, for the Branx
brig exists to this day, seemingly unchanged. Although the
bridge itself is heavily overgrown and concealed among a thick
band of vegetation running along both sides of the burn, its
connecting track is just discernible, if now virtually disused as
a result of the modern road that runs along the valley parallel
to the burn.

Following their ten-hour march through the drenched land-
scape the vanguard's forward units started to cross and work
their way up the Pallinsburn's southern slopes from where
they hoped to ascend the ridge of Branxton Hill and, after
negotiating its saddle, come upon the Scottish army. As yet
the visibility for the most forward units was extremely limited
due to vast clouds of smoke coming from the Scottish camp
that blew directly in their faces.

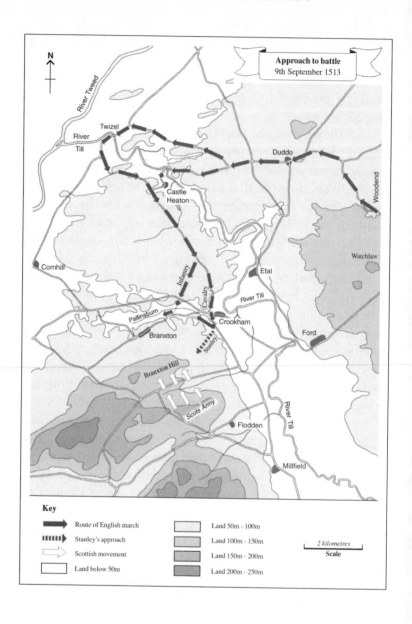

Approach to battle
9th September 1513

Key

- Route of English march
- Stanley's approach
- Scottish movement
- Land below 50m

- Land 50m - 100m
- Land 100m - 150m
- Land 150m - 200m
- Land 200m - 250m

2 kilometres
Scale

Unbeknown to them their opponents had also been active. During the evening of 8 September the Scots held their own council of war for which the only source of information is Robert Pitscottie's account; this, because of his undoubted bias and tendency to exaggerate, needs to be treated with care. From his description the meeting was a very lively affair. James IV, who had been on a reconnaissance to help gauge the options open to the English following their northward march, found on his return the nobles debating the situation and presently being addressed by Lord Patrick Lindsay (who happened to be Pitscottie's grandfather). Lindsay maintained that while they should keep their present formations their king, who was also leader of the largest division, must on no account be allowed to hazard his life in the anticipated battle. In his address Lindsay played on their emotions by likening them to an honest merchant about to play dice with a common gambler, in other words Surrey and his band of minor English nobles from the north. Far more important than such 'honest merchants', and infinitely more so than Surrey, was the Scottish king. He was 'a rose nobill' compared with that English 'bad halfpenny', 'an auld crooked earl lying in a chariot'.[4] James' nobles were, of course, quite correct in recognising the pivotal position of a feudal monarch in early sixteenth-century Scotland and especially that of James IV, but it was not a chivalrous discussion to the king's liking and – what was more – they were daring to suggest to him how he should order his battle.

He was said to have been enraged and vowed not only to fight 'this day with England' but to play his part to the full. He threatened to hang Lindsay for his presumption and, whether deliberately misrepresenting them or not, protested that though his lords might run away they would never shame him by making him do the same.[5] Such a reaction was entirely in character, for it was the king's zeal for action that had caused the Spanish ambassador to conclude in 1497 that 'he does not think it right to begin any warlike undertaking without being himself the first in danger'. Arguments raised by his magnates here or elsewhere that as a soldier he was worth just one man, whereas as a commander he might be worth a hundred thousand[6] had no effect. Quite apart from his personal inclinations, James was certain that only by showing himself in the thick of the fighting could he preserve the unity of a host containing such potential splinter groups as the Highlanders and Borderers. Whatever the arguments, the council achieved one purpose: following their seeming casualness when the English commenced their march, after the meeting of 8 September scouts were despatched to track every English move.

When the English ceased moving westward, crossed the river and turned southward towards Flodden, the Scottish commanders could no longer have any doubt about their intentions. James IV realised that if he allowed Surrey to climb Branxton Hill unopposed the English could not only obstruct his path back to Scotland but the move would also effectively reverse the earlier position between them. He must act quickly to frustrate it for, if he failed to transfer his army from Flodden Hill to Branxton Hill, he himself could easily be caught in the intervening saddle and any attack on the English would necessarily be uphill. The Scottish army had most likely been in a state of partial readiness since early that morning so that, when James' orders were given to move the mile and a half from Flodden Hill along the ridge to Branxton, they came as no great surprise. The greatest difficulties here were, of course, caused by their heavy guns. Their large ox teams would need skilful handling to drag the ordnance from their embrasures before moving them along the ridge. In the meantime, as tents were dismantled and divisions formed up, the heaps of rubbish accumulated by so many men and animals over the last few days were set on fire. This was customary practice for Scottish armies, although there has been much later conjecture about whether the 'great and marvellous smoke' was created deliberately to screen the army's movements. Intentional or not, it succeeded. Once the smoke cleared their new position would look down across a seemingly even descent to the lower crests guarding the Pallinsburn, from where they expected the English to come. High on the forward slopes they stood in a diamond shaped formation, four up and one in reserve, with each of the forward units just a bowshot distance from its neighbour.[7] The complement of the Scottish army, including the relative strengths of its formations is shown on the following page.

Meanwhile, the English forward units that crossed the Pallinsburn at about four o'clock in the afternoon were climbing out of the valley, still enveloped by the clouds of thick black smoke coming from the wet straw and other debris ignited by the Scots. After their slow progress so far the Admiral, anxious to establish his forces on Branxton Hill that day, hastened them on and as a consequence, apart from thin lines of soldiers beginning to man the southern crests, other units were scattered across the valley, with the bulk of the artillery still on the Pallinsburn's farther side. However, at about 4.15 a sudden squall of wind blew the smoke to one side and the men standing on the low tops beyond the Pallinsburn were terrified to see the whole of the Scottish army on Branxton Hill less than 600 metres away, from where a seemingly even slope stretched in their direction. They could make out four large divisions, their ranks tightly massed, and innumerable spearheads glistening in the fitful light. Between them stood massive artillery batteries and each soldier could easily have thought the guns' great barrels were pointing directly at him. Before the English had time to take in much more there were flashes, crashes and the roar of heavy projectiles as the cannon opened fire, while at the same time the Scottish long spears lowered in menacing fashion.

The Scottish Army at Flodden Commanded by James IV

Left Hand Division
10,000 strong
Joint Commanders: *Alexander, Lord Home and Alexander Gordon, Earl of Huntly*
The majority of men were Borderers from the Merse, Berwickshire and Roxburghshire regions.
Huntly's men, his own Gordons and other Highlanders from Aberdeenshire and Inverness-shire, were commanded by Gordon chieftains

Left Central Division
7000 strong
Joint Commanders: *William Hay, Earl of Errol, John Lindsay, Earl of Crawford, William Graham, Earl of Montrose*
Its soldiers were levies from Perthshire, Angus, Forfar, Fife and the other counties of the North-east Lowlands. Many Graham chieftains acted as its junior commanders

Main Battle
15,000 strong
To come under direct command of James IV.
Central were the Royal Household troops fighting under the banners of St Andrew and St Margaret. Circling these were the Scottish nobles without a command elsewhere, including the earls of Cassillis, Morton and Rothes, the lords Herries, Maxwell Innermeath, Borthwick and Sempill together with their semi-regular retainers.
Other troops came from the towns of Edinburgh, Ayr and Haddington, along with shire levies from Galloway and the Western Lowlands

Right Hand Division
5000 strong
Joint commanders: Archibald Campbell, Earl of Argyll and Matthew Stewart, Earl of Lennox.
All Highlanders with their chiefs, chieftains and heads of families, including Campbells of Glenorchy and Loudoun, Macleans of Duart, Mackenzies, Grants and some MacDonalds under McLean of Ardnamurchan. William Sinclair, Earl of Caithness, commanded the forces of Caithness, Sutherland and the Orkneys. Attached was the French knight d'Aussi with his 50 men-at-arms

Reserve Division (originally stationed on the extreme right but moved behind the Main Battle) 5000 strong
Commander *Adam Hepburn, Earl of Bothwell*
This consisted of probably the steadiest Lowland levies from the Lothians, the forest of Ettrick and from the Border burghs of Galashiels and Selkirk.

By the time of the battle these strength rolls were likely to have fallen by about 25% leaving the Scottish army with something like 30,000 men

CHAPTER TEN

≈

RIDING THE STORM

All armies have lived and marched amidst the unknown
Ferdinand Foch, *Precepts and Judgements*

AT THE ROAR of the first Scottish cannon the Admiral
knew that James had out-generalled him and his army was
placed in the greatest danger. Not only were the vanguard's
forward units still incomplete, but most of his light artillery –
his frail riposte to the highly imposing Scottish ordnance – had
still to be dragged across the narrow stone crossing of the Branx
brig, while his father's troops were even further to the rear. If
the Scots moved down upon him from Branxton Hill he would
surely be swept away. However, Thomas Howard did not lose
his head. He immediately moved his men back onto the reverse
slope, thereby not only protecting them from Scottish cannon
balls but concealing their weak state, and told his commanders
to position their soldiers in battle lines as they arrived.[1] Then
tearing off his sacred charm, the medallion of the Agnus Dei
or lamb of God, which he habitually kept round his neck for
divine protection, he threw it towards a horsed aid ordering
him to take it to his father to emphasise the need to come up
as quickly as possible, 'for the forward alone was not able to
encounter the whole battle of the Scots.'[2] He also moved his
men further down the valley to the right 'so that others could
move straight into line as they arrived and the vanguard and
rearguard might form a continuous front to the Scots.'[3]

His dramatic message was not lost on Surrey who drove
his weary troops forward to the sound of the Scottish guns.
According to tradition, most of the rearguard also crossed
the stream at the Branx brig, which played such a vital part
in helping the English concentrate their forces, although a

smaller number of soldiers, unwilling to await their turn at the bottleneck, worked their way round the eastern rim of the morass, from where they crossed the Pallinsburn before swinging back to fill their due places in the front lines. The crisis caused the English one major error of leadership. Surrey, in his anxiety to reach his son, either forgot to brief all his units about the new turn of events or failed to send guides to assist Stanley and his furthermost formation to join the forward lines. The result was that Stanley and his men only reached the battle when it was in its final stages, having approached the field by a longer and more circuitous route.

In spite of Surrey's lapse, together with his son he subsequently showed the coolness of mind needed by all effective battlefield commanders. On seeing the Scottish army in its four large divisions (the fifth placed in reserve was not apparent to them) they immediately set about reducing the number of their own divisions, the better to match those of their opponents. As the *Trewe Encountre* put it, 'Surrey and Lord Howard were constrained and enforced to divide their army in other four battles or else it was thought it should have been to their great danger and jeopardy.'[4]

To achieve this they broke up Dacre's right rearguard division except for his own 1500 horse and divided it among the others; the detachment of James Stanley, bishop of Ely, was added to Surrey's own formation, save for its Northumberland complement which reinforced Edmund Howard's division on the right of the line. Dacre's 1500 horse were ordered to act as a mobile reserve and 'stood apart by themselves to succour where most need was.' On the left Sir Marmaduke Constable's division was also dismantled with most of his troops going to increase the Admiral's contingent.

These were major changes and re-ordering formations on the field of battle has always been one of the most difficult of military exercises. The English had to carry out this re-ordering after two days of continuous marching, and the reallocation had to be accomplished while they crouched behind a shallow slope as massive cannon balls, against which they seemed to have no adequate response, were flying over their heads. Nonetheless, they succeeded in forming three larger divisions, not including Sir Edward Stanley with his 3500 tenants from his family's estate, who had yet to join them. Significantly, all three forward divisions were commanded by Howards, the right-hand one by Edmund, the central and largest by the Admiral, and the left-hand one by Surrey himself.

With the re-ordering complete and with pairs or even small batteries of guns brought up between the formations, orders were given to stand up and climb out of the Pallinsburn valley. Moving forward on open ground dominated by an enemy occupying its higher slopes 'both [the Admiral's and Surrey's] wards advanced against the Scots.' They were soon halted and, as their accompanying artillery commenced its counter-firing, the troops had no option but to stand in easy range of the much more powerful Scottish cannon and look nervously at the larger numbers of Scots looking down on them some 600 metres away. The brutally long marches of the last two days had undoubtedly achieved their commander's aim; they had brought the Scots to battle. Whether there was a chance of defeating them was, of course, quite another matter. Not only were the Scottish cannon far superior but, with Stanley's division absent, they were plainly outmatched numerically, and after so much effort to reach the ground many of the sodden men were very weary and in places morale was not at its highest.

The Cheshire men, under Edmund Howard, were terror-stricken by their first experience of artillery fire and cowered below the crest of the Pallinsburn slopes with 'white faces and trembling limbs'.[5] When during the initial artillery exchanges just one of the heavy Scottish cannon balls dropped close to Dacre's 'prickers' from Bamburgh and Tynemouth, they panicked and rode off the field. They happened to be standing close to Edmund Howard's men whose morale was thereby

dealt another heavy blow. Fortunately for the English, however, such behaviour was far from general; most wanted to
fight and they would fight.

Conditions appeared more favourable for the Scottish army.
While the enveloping smoke from their fires had prevented
the English from following their progress along the ridge
from Flodden to Branxton, their own scouts had succeeded
in keeping the English under close observation from the time
they crossed the River Till until they neared Branxton. The
English predicament caused by the wet ground guarding the
Pallinsburn and their need to cross it at the Branx brig was also
known to the Scottish commanders. This had caused James
IV's master gunner to approach him and ask permission to
bombard them at the choke points on both sides of the Branx
brig, before they climbed out of the valley. But his request
was refused, which Pitscottie considered to be the action
of 'a man bereft of his wit.'[6] The manner of James' reply,
however, was far from uncalculating. The Scots' ammunition
and powder were not limitless and he told Robert Borthwick,
'I am determined. I will have them all before me on a plain
field and essay them what they can do before me.'

Some commentators have attributed such a reply to the
king's misplaced sense of chivalry, but the likelier explanation
is that he was unwilling to use his relatively crude artillery
and restricted quantities of powder and ammunition at long
range against a target considerably less favourable than English
battle lines standing some 600 metres away. He also had good
reasons not to release his army against an English vanguard
spread throughout the Pallinsburn valley, whose rough slopes
presented difficulties for pike columns which were all too
likely to lose cohesion and become vulnerable themselves.
In hindsight it can be seen that James probably lost a great
opportunity here but his Border 'prickers', who would have
been invaluable in such a role, had by now been converted
into pike columns.

Just as James had felt safe on Flodden Hill where the English would have been compelled to attack uphill into the mouths of his guns, he knew well that after emerging from the wide valley of the Pallinsburn they would need to cross open slopes before reaching his position fronting the crest of Branxton Hill. Most importantly, James would have anticipated a major battle-winning role for his artillery when, after waiting for the English to come into his guns' field of fire he could blast their massed formations away as they toiled upwards.

For these reasons James did not try to prevent the English forming into their battle line: this was the opportunity he had looked for since as a youth he had watched his great cannon pound castles to rubble. By engaging in an artillery duel before their main clash of arms both sides were moving into the military unknown – but it was James IV who was most surprised by the turn of events. In what he could reasonably have anticipated would be an uneven duel between his guns and the English ordnance, things rapidly went wrong. Although the discharges of the Scottish guns were terrifyingly loud to English levies unused to such weapons, and their massive projectiles aroused fearful wonder, they failed to tear bloody corridors through the English formations as expected; in fact, 'our bullets . . . but flew over their heads.'[7] The Scottish historian, John Lesley, was quite specific on this point, although Niall Barr thinks the Scottish gunners would have had little difficulty in laying their rounds on the English troops, and it was probably the soft ground that explained such relatively little damage. This could doubtless have applied to the few rounds that fell among the more open English formations but, in the vast majority of cases, the Scottish guns were well off target. In fact, the Chronicler Edward Hall was utterly dismissive of them saying, 'They did no harm to the English army.' A number of factors contributed to such disastrous results from the Scottish point of view, all stemming from the need to fire downhill. Lacking trunions by which they could elevate or depress their gun barrels from the horizontal, the whole gun carriages (to which the barrels were securely attached) had to be angled accordingly. To lower their aim they had to dig the guns' wheels into the ground. But positioned on the soft ground just down from the summit of Branxton Hill – and having no anti-recoil equipment – at the moment of firing the guns would have tended to jerk backwards and upwards, thus raising their angle of shot. Placing them on wooden platforms would have helped offset this, but these were very cumbersome. They were unlikely to have been brought from Flodden and there was certainly no time to find and assemble the materials needed to build new platforms on the battlefield. What time there was would most likely have been spent erecting some degree of protection.

Apart from the problems caused by the soft and downward sloping ground an additional one arose from the need to calculate the parabolic trajectory of the more powerful Scottish guns. (The lighter and straighter firing English ones being aimed uphill had no such problem.) This could have been solved by firing sighting rounds but for a number of reasons, not least the certainty of revealing the Scottish army's new positions, it did not happen.

Finally, however important these factors were in the initial inaccuracy of the Scottish ordnance they had little opportunity to sort things out on the field of battle before a storm of shot from the English guns began to shatter their weapons and maim their crews.

The fact was that Robert Borthwick and his largely inexperienced gunners faced a strange and confusing situation and it was not until the next century that the great Swedish general Gustavus Adolphus (1596–1634) adapted artillery for the quite different roles of besieging castles and fighting opposing forces by making his field units mobile. At Flodden the heavy Scottish artillery – whether or not they used their sixty pounders – with its high proportion of oxen, was not that easy to move, especially across country, and its teams had accomplished marvels dragging it from Flodden to Branxton Hill. The unexpected problems of downward firing were

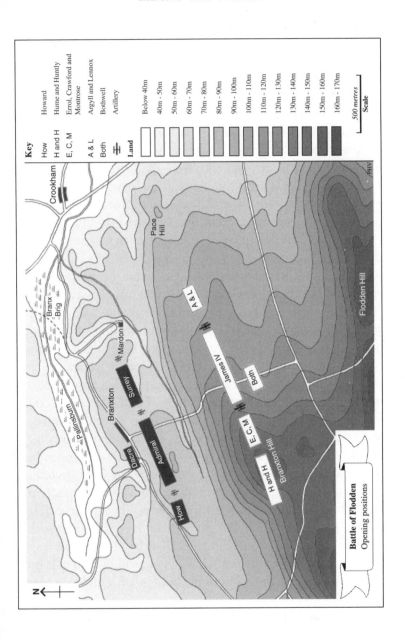

Key

How	Howard	
H and H	Hume and Huntly	
E, C, M	Errol, Crawford and Montrose	
A & L	Argyll and Lennox	
Both	Bothwell	
Land	Artillery	

Below 40m
40m – 50m
50m – 60m
60m – 70m
70m – 80m
80m – 90m
90m – 100m
100m – 110m
110m – 120m
120m – 130m
130m – 140m
140m – 150m
150m – 160m
160m – 170m

500 metres
Scale

Battle of Flodden
Opening positions

compounded by the performance of the English artillery which, so much lighter and manoeuvrable, proved far more potent than could have been expected. It not only enjoyed the immense advantage of being able to fire uphill but its handlers also proved highly competent, not only firing faster, which was only to be expected, but with remarkable accuracy. Hall wrote triumphantly that their shot 'slew the Master Gunner of Scotland and beat all his men from their ordnance',[8] although in fact Robert Borthwick survived Flodden and cast many church bells afterwards,[9] but many other Scottish gun captains and their teams were either killed or fled from their guns. In trained hands and with conditions in their favour, derisory two-pounder falcons proved themselves more deadly than their massive opponents. This brought remarkable benefits for, when the Scottish fire dropped away the English were able to switch their targeting upon the tightly massed Scottish columns, where a single ball could down any man, however well-armoured, and on its continuing flight lop off heads or limbs from others. Such fire was a new experience for most of them and all the more terrifying as a consequence.

James IV therefore found himself in a position not unlike the one he had planned for the English. He faced a force that could remain where it was and still batter him to defeat. Admittedly Surrey did advance his divisions just beyond Branxton village, but this only forced the Scots to depress their guns even further, and the English halted before a marshy hollow stretching across the field with a stream that would help impede any Scottish movement towards them. Surrey had absolutely no reason to move while his guns continued to scourge his opponents' dense columns, in particular the magnificent target presented by the largest Scottish division, where Hall tells how the guns shot 'into the midst of the King's battle and slew many persons'.[10]

With James, it was different. Like the unfortunate Charles Edward Stuart at Culloden more than two centuries later, his men could not go on enduring such fire. He had three options.

The first was to move his units back onto the reverse slope below the crest of Branxton Hill from where he could await an English attack upon which his men could jump up and drive back their opponents. Such a withdrawal would inevitably be difficult for his army's morale and impossible for his cumbrous guns and, in any case, it was against all his instincts. The second option was to attack himself. The third and unthinkable one was to refuse battle altogether.

Understandably James opted for the second option, relying on the downward slopes from Branxton Hill to give his 'state of the art' pike columns the necessary momentum to smash through the waiting English formations. But this would not satisfy James. While, as a renaissance monarch, he might seek military success through the most recent developments in weaponry, he remained traditional in believing the true place for a Scottish monarch was at the front. Shortly after despatching his vanguard he ordered his horse to the rear, took up a pike, led his household troops to the forward ranks of his division, and called on his noblemen to join him. Magnificent as it was, this deprived the Scottish army of its supreme leader for, hemmed in among the front ranks, James would be unable to see any developments occurring elsewhere and would be powerless to respond appropriately. However, the urge to attack was implicit in Scottish military traditions and, allied with good timing, it had proved a successful tactic for both William Wallace and Robert Bruce. In the early sixteenth century, in spite of the new prominence given to the cavalry, pike columns like those of James were still the most potent weapons of war and, in any case, the English had no genuine cavalry to pit against them.

Moreover James was, as we have seen, convinced that only by showing himself in the thick of the fray could he keep his heterogeneous army together. As he took up his position the decisive and most bloody stage of the campaign was about to begin.

≈

CHAPTER ELEVEN

FIGHT TO THE DEATH

Fascination with new technology but lack of skill in using it
Norman MacDougall, *James IV*

FOLLOWING A BLAST of trumpets and commands from their Gallic drill sergeants the three main phalanxes of Scottish spearmen commenced their attack. As yet uncommitted was the division of Highlanders under the joint command of Lennox and Argyll, holding their traditional station on the right flank, and the Scottish reserve formation, under the Earl of Bothwell. Opposing the Scottish attackers, from left to right, were the three English divisions under Edmund Howard the Admiral and Surrey himself. Dacre's 1500 light cavalry were stationed in the rear while Stanley's division was yet to reach the battle area.

From its leftmost position the Scottish vanguard was the first to move, with Home's Borderers in their spear formations and Huntly's Highlanders loping along on their flanks. Unlike earlier conflicts, the Scots are described as coming down the hill silently, 'after the Almayns manner'[1] as their French trainers had instructed them. Whether this was more frightening to the waiting troops than shouting out their clan cries or invocations to their favoured saints is debatable, but despite the slipperiness of the ground, most kept their tight formations and moved their heavy spears to forward-facing as they neared the English positions. Following European practice, divisions were scheduled to advance in echelon formation in order to strike their opponent with rapidly succeeding blows, but whether this was more telling than the traditional Scottish practice of delivering a single fearsome punch is again highly debatable. For the echelon system to be fully effective precise timing was vital, in other words following the impact made by the first assaulting formation the second had to crash onto its appointed target before help could be given to the beleaguered defenders, and for this sequence to be repeated all along the line. Ideally this rippling effect would prove devastating. However, if the follow-up divisions suffered delays the whole assault was bound to be compromised and the defenders afforded the chance to regroup or even provide mutual support. Due to the varying conformation of the ground from the crest of Branxton Hill to the English positions and the difficult conditions underfoot, such accurate timing was virtually impossible. Careful pre-reconnaissance should have revealed such ground variations and the need for appropriate tactical adjustment: therefore the question has to be asked whether, in their haste to leave Flodden Hill, the Scottish leaders neglected to do this, or whether the smoke that partially obscured the slopes made it too late for them to conduct a thorough survey of the ground.

The vanguard was by far the most fortunate of the attacking Scottish formations as it faced a relatively even slope before clashing with Edmund Howard's waiting forces. In spite of the difficulty of staying upright in the deep clinging mud they kept their formations intact, with Huntly's Highlanders, bows ready or two-handed swords drawn, providing vital protection on the flanks. The Highlanders were, of course, accustomed to marching barefooted and this so helped their footing that many of the attacking Borderers also discarded their footwear. From his position higher on Branxton Hill James IV watched the vanguard's silent, ordered progress in delight. If this were maintained the English could scarcely withstand them.

As luck would have it, the vanguard was opposed by much the weakest English formation, a mixed unit of 3000 men, (belatedly supplemented in the Pallinsburn valley by a further 1000 men from Northumberland) and commanded, not by the most senior Howards, but by the Admiral's relatively unknown and untried younger brother, Edmund. The initial force was

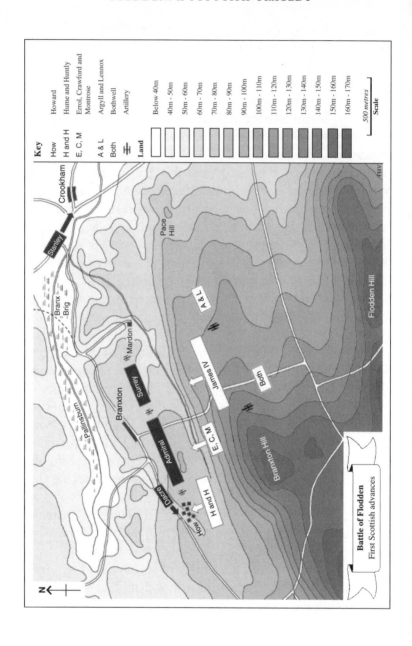

Key

How	Howard
H and H	Hume and Huntly
E, C, M	Errol, Crawford and Montrose
A & L	Argyll and Lennox
Both	Bothwell
☩	Artillery
Land	

Below 40m
40m – 50m
50m – 60m
60m – 70m
70m – 80m
80m – 90m
90m – 100m
100m – 110m
110m – 120m
120m – 130m
130m – 140m
140m – 150m
150m – 160m
160m – 170m

500 metres
Scale

Battle of Flodden
First Scottish advances

made up of levies from Cheshire, Lancashire and Yorkshire, stiffened by a 200-strong contingent provided by the Admiral and commanded by Maurice Berkeley, captain of the ship the *Mary George*. This force had been the first to come under fire from the Scottish cannon and it had also been forced to wait the longest while other English formations came into line.

To the waiting levies the advancing phalanx must have been a daunting spectacle, with its banners flying and the flamboyant and well-armed Highlanders on its flanks. At its core the massed spears were so long and dense that their handlers' faces were obscured and to the defenders it might have seemed as if they were moving forward of their own volition – suggesting they could not be stopped. Facing such weight of numbers and doubting whether they could ever bring their bills close enough to do their enemies any damage, Howard's men quickly showed signs of wavering.

James and his accompanying knights watched as individual soldiers began leaving Edmund Howard's lines to be joined by gathering numbers of panic-stricken men, including some knights and their households, running to the rear. The English battle line broke into detached clusters of men in which officers and sergeants struggled to restore some sort of defensive formation before the attackers were upon them. James' bitter disappointment over his artillery was forgotten. Here was proof his new spear formations would carry the day. Whatever the plans of his French instructors for echeloning, the momentum had to be kept going at all costs: the Lowland levies of Errol, Crawford and Montrose's division next in line must give immediate support and he and his own magnificent column must support a unified attack which would drive Surrey and his men backward into the marshland of the Pallinsburn valley.

After James joined the forward units his advisers unavailingly told him a king was not rashly 'to enter the fight, but to provide and see that everything is done in order.'[2] Had not Robert Bruce's essential contribution to the Scottish victory at Bannockburn been his ability to read the battle, to anticipate every English move and successfully to counter it? Such arguments made no impression upon James, a relatively inexperienced but intensely proud commander, whose warlike dreams and chivalric ideals dictated that his rightful place must be at the head of his men. To place himself in such jeopardy was serious enough, but it was compounded by his failure to appoint a deputy and to omit issuing orders to his Highlanders on the extreme right of his line or to his reserve under Adam Hepburn, Earl of Bothwell. Notwithstanding, if the Scots' follow-up divisions could match the controlled momentum of their vanguard there seemed an excellent chance of seizing victory.

In reality, when battle was joined the best Scottish expectations for their vanguard were not to be realised. Although many of the English levies had melted away before the daunting sight of the advancing spear columns, some isolated groups continued to stand firm. There were even instances of offensive action. Bryan Tunstall of Thurland, ashamed of the cowardice around him, after kneeling down and taking a small portion of earth in his mouth as a last communion, launched himself at the advancing enemy, killing a Scottish knight before being cut down by many hands. Other contingents, like that of Maurice Berkeley, saw their leader killed fighting in the front rank, while virtually the entire Macclesfield unit was killed, together with their commander, Christopher Savage. Other courageous captains, such as Thomas Venables and Robert Fouleshurst, were killed driving their Cheshire men back into the fight. Sir John Booth and John Lawrence died rallying their Lancashire levies, while the young Robert Warcop and Sir William Fitzwilliam died when, with their fellow Yorkshiremen, they vainly tried to halt the advancing pikemen and were overrun.

In such conditions the Scottish spear formations loosened and the fighting deteriorated into a series of isolated engagements which mainly went in favour of the Scots. Amazingly, Edmund Howard found himself virtually alone, except for his standard-bearer and two retainers, and his life was probably saved by the Borderers' hopes for ransom. They captured his standard-bearer and hewed him in pieces but, although struck to the ground three times, Edmund managed to keep hold of his sword and continued to beat off his attackers.[3] Although the youngest of the Howards was soon to offer further evidence of his fighting ability, nothing could change the fact that his force had been virtually destroyed and a dangerous gap made in the left of the English line.

Meanwhile, James IV's orders had brought his second division of pike-carrying levies into contention, commanded by three of his great magnates, the earls of Errol, Crawford and Montrose. Unlike Home's and Huntly's division, they were unable to move straight downward towards their opponents, since fronting their target was a small stream followed by an uphill climb before they could close upon the Admiral's division on the forward edge of Piper's hill. In addition, their task, if not impossible, was far more difficult than that of the vanguard, since their 6000 men were heavily outnumbered by the Admiral's 10,000 men. Their attack might have stood a good chance of success if only Home's and Huntly's force had quickly followed up their success by moving eastward to roll up the Admiral's division from the flank. But, unlike the Scottish king, Surrey remained in firm control and it was entirely likely that he issued the orders for Lord Dacre and his 1500 border cavalry to bolster Howard's shattered formation into continuing to oppose the Scottish vanguard.

Although heavily outnumbered, Dacre's mobile 'border pickers' did not disappoint him. In fact they came into their own, fighting in traditional fashion by targeting their opponents' leaders. With their lances and bolts from their crossbows they transfixed three of Home's cousins and other border lairds, such as the Crichtons, Cockburns, Douglases, Kerrs and Bromfields, together with four of the Highland chieftains. However, they suffered significant losses of their own from the pikes of their opponents. Dacre lost some

160 killed and three of his commanders, Philip Dacre, Sir Humphrey Lyle and Harry Gray, were taken prisoner.

Meanwhile amid the confused and bitter fighting the bastard John Heron of Ford, with a small cavalry vedette, succeeded in slashing his way through the Scottish ranks to rescue Edmund Howard although he himself was seriously wounded in the process. As they struggled back towards the Admiral's division their way was blocked by Sir Davy Home, whom Edmund Howard killed in single combat.

Gallant as such isolated instances of resistance were, it was the attack by the border prickers that effectively prevented Home from giving the Scottish second division the support it so sorely needed. Dacre fully occupied the vanguard's attention and so bloody did the encounter become that it ended with a deliberate stand-off as both sides blew their trumpets and 'convened their men again to their standards'.[4] Not only did Home fail to assist the second division of Scottish attackers, but he withdrew his men up Branxton Hill leaving Dacre holding its lower reaches. Most of Home's and Dacre's men were Borderers and, with the complicated tapestry of inter-border relationships and feuds that prevailed at the time, it is quite possible that both sides came to a mutual decision that they had done enough. Niall Barr, for one, discounts this in his belief 'that both the Scots and English on this flank were fought out and incapable of indulging in more fighting'[5] and Dacre, of course, strongly denies there was ever such an arrangement. However, the casualty levels, while considerable, do not fully support them being fought out, although both sides unquestionably lost close kinsmen. Pitscottie brings further attention to the self-seeking nature of the Borderers by recounting a later incident in the battle when James IV seemed hard pressed and Huntly wanted to help, but Home refused on the grounds that, 'He does well for himself. We have fought our vanguard already and won the same therefore let the rest do their part as well as we.'[6]

Any such accommodation between the Borderers from both

sides undoubtedly helped the English cause more than the Scots'. Home and Huntly failed their king by losing any chance of mounting a dangerous flank attack against the Admiral, while Dacre's much smaller force achieved its purpose of stabilising the English line as well as continuing to provide a screen for its right flank. Such lack of support from Home and Huntly meant the second division's attack upon much superior English forces was virtually bound to fail and go far to costing James IV his victory.

Whatever criticisms might be levelled against James IV's leadership at Flodden, he undoubtedly succeeded in despatching his second division upon the heels of the vanguard and by his personal example galvanising his own division into following close upon them. The second division launched its attack probably fifteen minutes after the early signs of English panic, and although few details survive, the heroism with which it was conducted cannot be doubted. The attackers apparently succeeded in maintaining their tight schiltron formation until their progress was interrupted by the small stream, which was to prove so important, running across their front. This presented a quite unexpected obstacle and it was followed by a daunting if relatively short climb before they could get among the English astride the conical feature of Piper's Hill. The stream is difficult to see from the top of Branxton Hill and from there the small eminence of Piper's Hill looks nothing like the obstacle it proved to be. It needs little imagination to realise the problems of Errol, Crawford and Montrose: the small stream had cut a deep path between rocky outcrops which would compel the spear columns to compress themselves in a concertina-like movement. Once across, the forward movement could only be resumed with difficulty as the foremost spearmen struggled upward under a hail of missiles. The battlefield observers had no doubt the attackers were affected by 'the unevenness of the hill',[7] which also gave the English opportunities to mount flank attacks against pikemen impeded by their overlong weapons; those who discarded their pikes then found themselves facing English bill-hooks that outranged their swords. This time there was no wavering on the part of the defenders, nor with their superior numbers should there have been. With 'pure fighting' the Admiral's professional soldiers zestfully scythed into their enemies and killed so many that they eventually broke and scattered all over the field. Their horrendous casualties included all three co-commanders, and elsewhere in the formation it was said 'no less than eighty-seven Hays fell around Errol, the head of their clan.'[8] In contrast the English casualties were relatively light.

Scottish hopes now rested on their massive central division led by the king, almost double the strength of Surrey's soldiers directly opposing it. Setting off shortly after the second division it too had the stream to cross, followed by a rise on the further side, but here the ground beyond the stream was somewhat straighter than at Piper's Hill. In any case the tall and well-armoured 'personages' in its forward ranks succeeded in maintaining better progress, although nothing like the rate of momentum anticipated across what had been thought was an even field. Coming down the hill this formation would have presented a remarkable sight: over most of the short journey its dense thicket of advancing pikes could justly have seemed invincible, while over its front ranks there floated a forest of brightly coloured banners, some of them five yards long, the king himself being flanked by the crimson and gold of the banner royal, together with the sacred blue banners of St Margaret and St Andrew. In the forward battle lines were not only the king and his household knights, but a large group of other nobles wearing full armour with metal sallets on their heads, shut down to protect their faces from the English longbows. James himself was clad in a magnificent suit of armour surmounted by a gold and scarlet surcoat bearing the royal arms of Scotland, and on his finger he wore the turquoise ring sent him by the Queen of France. In the foremost ranks the knights were carrying heavy wooden shields (pavises) for protection against

English arrows in addition to their pikes and other personal weapons.

On this occasion the English longbow did not prove nearly as deadly as before: the combination of pavises and armour went far to blunting its effect; and in fact one observer remarked that with the Scottish front ranks equipped 'with complete harneys, jacks, almayn, ryvettes, spletes, pavices and other habilimentes that shote of arrowes in regarde did thaim no harme.'9 The English archers were also hampered by the rain and strong wind blowing in their faces but, in spite of such problems, the showers of arrows unleashed by them succeeded in wounding the less well protected men in the rearward columns. Armour, of course, provided no protection against the artillery firing at point-blank range into the solid masses of attackers as they charged the last few yards towards the waiting English.

In spite of such deadly missiles and the irregularities of the ground, to its immense credit the king's division kept reasonable order as it moved resolutely forwards. In theory with its numbers it had the ability to punch through the weaker English units, following which it could move against the defenders from the flanks and rear. In practice, the experienced English soldiers deliberately gave ground, in places up to 200 yards, and the main blow fell upon Surrey's 500 veteran retainers, supported by George Darcy's company to their left. While the English line undoubtedly bent it did not break, and by so giving ground it created a dangerous pocket for the attacker: as the Scottish advance slowed, and then stopped altogether, the English soldiers found their eight-foot bills excellent killing tools against the attackers' vulnerable flanks. These heavy-headed weapons scythed into their armoured opponents whose swords for the most part could make no effective reply. Amongst the first Scottish soldiers to fall were the lords Maxwell and Herries. Unwittingly or not, by giving ground the English had adopted a classic battle-winning formation and, while Surrey's men were not strong enough to exploit it fully, the Admiral came to his father's aid with his formation smashing into the unprotected left flank of the king's pike columns.

The battle turned into a vicious hand-to-hand struggle that continued for two hours or more with the English bills inflicting frightful injuries as their spikes sought out vulnerable faces and their sharp axe blades hewed off limbs. Over the muddy, stream-crossed hills of Northumberland the Scottish king's new weapons of war, on which he had set so much store, failed him: the guns had proved useless when having to fire downhill and the French-inspired spear columns had been brought to a halt. Everything now hinged on which side could keep going the longest and whose hand weapons would prove most effective, although there was also the vital question of whether any forces so far uncommitted could wrest back the advantage for their side. Here the Scots appeared to have clear advantages. Whereas a single English division under Sir Edward Stanley had yet to approach the field of battle, the Scottish reserve was still uncommitted and a further division of Highlanders, under Argyll and Lennox, stood on their hill-top to the right of the Scottish line. The latter were capable of moving quickly and their two-handed swords could be expected to make a telling effect.

The full facts are not altogether clear but it seems that, when the king's division appeared to be getting the worst of things, the Scottish reserve under Bothwell moved round and started reinforcing it from the rear. No commentator at the time of the battle suggests the king ordered Bothwell forward to assist him, for James and his household troops were probably so heavily involved in defending themselves that no messenger was sent. The likelihood is that Bothwell committed the reserve on his own initiative. Unfortunately, his intervention was not best directed. By feeding his 5000 fine Lowland pikemen into the rear of a pocket he was reinforcing what was rapidly becoming a disaster. If Bothwell had been able to direct them in a concerted attack against Surrey's left flank where it overlapped the king's division it might have been different.

Contrastingly, for several reasons, the Highlanders watching the costly struggle from their eminence did not move quickly to their king's support. Several explanations have been put forward for this: there may have been internal disputes over their best course of action, for not everyone was enthusiastic over supporting a rash Lothian king in what was increasingly looking like a losing cause; they might simply have been confused because James had failed to give them any instructions, and to complicate things further the French Count d'Aussi certainly tried to dissuade them from charging down the hill in support of the king's division. Whatever the reason, a fatal hesitation occurred. Finally, from the pattern of the fighting between the two swaying battle lines and the diminishing number of Scottish banners, the king's position so clearly appeared to be worsening that differences were put aside and the Highland chiefs prepared to move their powerful division down from the hill to help tilt the balance in their king's favour. Disastrously for the Scots they were prevented from doing so by the last English formation to enter the battle.

The sequence of events was as follows. Since Sir Edward Stanley's division was always rearmost of the English forces, it would have experienced fearful difficulties fording the Till at Heaton Mill after the steep banks there had been thoroughly churned up by the earlier detachments. Moreover, lacking local guides it had probably become further detached from the main body, and being ignorant of the Pallinsburn's crossing place by the Branx brig, Stanley was likely to have led his men down the road skirting the Pallinsburn morass through the small hamlet of Crookham, where he might have been told about the Highlanders' position at the right of the Scottish line. From Crookham he almost certainly crossed the burn at Sandyford, from where he could work his way up the north-eastern corner of Pace Hill towards the Highlanders who, Stanley rightly concluded, might be about to relieve the 'King of Scots' Battle'.[10]

Stanley and his men had been marching for over eleven hours in testing conditions but they were still full of fight and determined to take a major part in the contest. He led them up the hill's slopes, slopes so steep, in fact, that they 'were forced on hands and feet to creep'[11] in order to surprise the Highlanders on the summit. When on the summit, Stanley's men massed their archers and poured clouds of arrows into the Scots' backs. It was not just the surprising nature of the manoeuvre that made it effective but also the fact that the Highlanders, unlike other Scottish divisions, were, with the exception of their mail shirts, largely unprotected from arrows. While the arrows were finding their targets, Stanley formed up his men-at-arms and billmen on the Highlanders' right flank, under the leadership of Sir William Molyneux, Sir Thomas Gerrard and Sir Henry Kighley; they waited until the Highlanders could no longer stand firm against the deadly shafts and then all three English formations charged at them.[12] Upon this the Highlanders fled in all directions and their two co-commanders, the earls of Argyll and Lennox, together with Lord Darnley and the clan chiefs Campbell of Glenorchy, McIan of Ardnamurchan and Maclean, were killed 'doing all they could to stay their people from running away.'[13]

With the opening of fighting on the right flank, James realised he now had little or no chance of rapid reinforcements from this source and, with Home and Huntly seemingly unwilling to leave their position on the left, the chances of a powerful intervention from there were exceedingly slim. With the Scottish and English flanking divisions out of the equation, the numbers of men engaged in the centre were relatively similar and both sides fought on with the pride and determination of their race. The Scots had been instructed by their French trainers not to shout and the fight was conducted with a cold and silent fury.[14] Close-quarter exchanges of this nature were not only a savage but a most exhausting process, for the energy used in holding and directing a fifteen-foot spear, swinging an eight-foot bill or engaging in the slash and thrust of sword play is massive. The Scots might have been thought to have the advantage in such exchanges as they were relatively fresh and better fed, but clad in bulky undergarments topped by confining armour many in the king's division became exhausted. In any case during such primeval exchanges the English bill was proving superior to the assorted weapons of the Scots, and as bravely as the Scottish king and the vast majority of his followers conducted themselves (it is claimed that James killed five men with his spear before having it broken in his hands[15]), they were gradually being beaten.

Even when all reasonable hope seemed to have died James IV refused to accept defeat. He reasoned that if he could only kill the English commander his opponents might still lose hope and so, gathering his household troops and as many others as he could, he embarked on a desperate charge towards Surrey's banners. He crashed through the forward English ranks but as his force suffered casualties the weight of his attack slackened; when his banner-bearer was killed at the king's side the proud Stewart finally had to accept the only way to save himself from the reproach that would follow was in death. He ran headlong into the thick of his enemies, fighting in a most desperate manner, where he was beaten down and slain. The extent of his endeavour can be appreciated by the fact that he fell a mere spear's length from his adversary, Surrey, with an arrow piercing his lower jaw and his throat slashed from ear to ear by a brown bill.[16] With the king died his son, the Archbishop of St Andrews, the earls of Bothwell, Cassillis, Morton and many others.

At first few realised the king was lost, but when Argyll and Lennox's Highlanders in their flight from Stanley's men ran down from their hill and across the field of battle, they passed the bodies of the Scottish king and his household. They were themselves saved from probable death as their pursuers caught sight of the rich garments lying on the grass and 'fell on . . . and spoiled the King of Scots and many that were slain in his battle, but they knew him not.'[17] When the king's banners

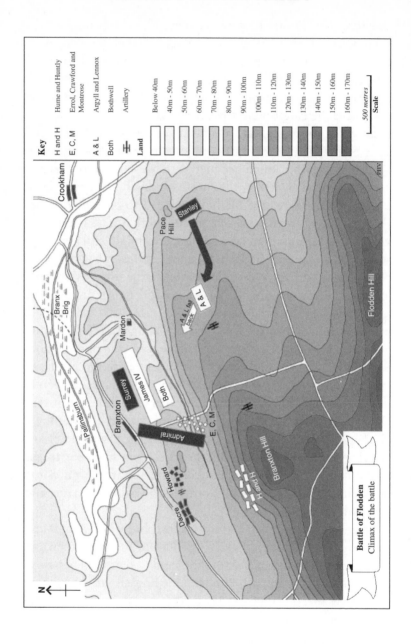

Battle of Flodden
Climax of the battle

Key

H and H	Hume and Huntly
E, C, M	Errol, Crawford and Montrose
A & L	Argyll and Lennox
Both	Bothwell
	Artillery

Below 40m
40m - 50m
50m - 60m
60m - 70m
70m - 80m
80m - 90m
90m - 100m
100m - 110m
110m - 120m
120m - 130m
130m - 140m
140m - 150m
150m - 160m
160m - 170m
Land

500 metres
Scale

could no longer be seen the Scots were forced to accept the unthinkable that their king was probably dead, and with the collective will of their great undertaking taken from them it was said they did not know what to do.[18] Some fled back to Scotland, crossing the Tweed by the fords near Coldstream, by Wark Castle or Lennel near Cornhill Castle or by the dry marches further west,[19] while other proud men fought on in spite of the hopelessness of their cause. Few who offered to surrender on the field of battle were successful for, as the Admiral promised the Scottish king prior to the fighting, they would take no prisoners because 'they were soe vengeable and cruell in their feighting that when Englishmen had the better of thaim they wold not save thaim.'[20]

The slaughtering went on until approximately seven o'clock in the evening when it grew dark, and as the Scottish numbers dwindled the English billmen were able to concentrate on killing the heavily armoured nobles, strong and great men who in magnificent obstinacy 'would not fall when four or five bill struck on them at once.'[21] Elsewhere the English Borderers characteristically intent on booty made for the Scottish camp where they slit the throats of the retainers and other followers, plundered and drove away draught oxen and thousands of horses.[22]

On the main field no general order was given for the fighting to stop and Surrey did not leave it until his aides had assured him the Scots seemed quite incapable of fresh offensive action, and not before he had knighted forty of his officers, including his younger son, Edmund. After placing strong guards under command of Sir Philip Tilney on both his own and the Scottish artillery, he left the hillside bestrewn with its dead where his soldiers were still despatching the wounded and rode back to the relative peace of Bar moor wood, where he had camped the night before.[23] Surrey had already sent news of his victory south but at Bar moor his son, the Lord Admiral, sent off a full dispatch to Queen Catherine. In fact the English successes were not quite unbroken, for in the twilight some soldiers intent on pursuit ran into superior numbers of retreating Scots and were themselves captured.[24] Other Englishmen, some no doubt impeded by their wounded, followed Surrey to Bar moor but were incensed to find their tents plundered and their personal possessions and horses stolen. With the Scots in such disarray they strongly suspected the English Borderers and many vowed that, successful as the day had been, they would never return to the area.

The next morning saw another instance of Border opportunism when a body of 800 horsemen, almost certainly under the direction of Lord Home, looked likely to overwhelm the relatively small escort placed over the captured Scottish artillery. However, the Admiral was at hand and the English master gunner, William Brackenall, fired a salvo in their direction which put them to flight.[25] In fact, the Borderers represented the only offensive formations left in Scotland, for under their aged commander the northern English levies had gained an overwhelming victory. James' proud Scottish army, which at his summons had come from across the face of Scotland, had been destroyed.

Estimates of casualties are notoriously difficult and, despite English eye-witnesses putting the numbers of Scottish dead as high as 15,000–17,000, it seems safe to conclude they were closer to 10,000 men, still an amazing third of their total force. In comparison Hall acknowledged 1500 English casualties with none of their senior leaders killed. Such casualties were far from the whole story: many of the Scottish soldiers who survived the fighting subsequently died while escaping, a number of them in the fords across a swollen Tweed.[26] With such high Scottish casualties Polydore Vergil was less than generous in describing such terrorised and hungry men as living pariahs in their own land, because 'bewildered and forgetful of their duty they had not attempted either to avenge the death of the King or to help their comrades in their extremity and so had branded their country with everlasting shame.'[27] Many such men had to pillage their own country before reaching home.

As significant as the number of the losses were those included among the dead. By far the most important casualty, of course, was the king himself, the most successful monarch from his line who not only brought unity and prosperity to Scotland but sought to raise its status among the other countries in Europe. The king's body, naked like most of the others, was not found until the morning after the battle, when it was recovered and brought from the field by two of his servants who had been captured and were compelled to accompany Lord Dacre (who knew James well) in a search of the battlefield.[28] Together with the king fell two bishops, two mitred abbots, twelve earls, thirteen lords and five eldest sons of peers, as well as at least 300 of Scotland's most influential nobility, both clergy and gentry. Virtually every family of note was deprived of a relative and a whole generation of rulers and administrators was lost.

Such casualties help to illustrate the quality and commitment of the army James IV assembled for his thrust into England which – unforgivably – he made as much for personal reasons as for vital interests of state, and which, as we know, came to follow the tragic pattern of so many earlier forays south. Despite the strength of the Scottish army in 1513, what proved decisive was the marked singleness of purpose and superior leadership of the English compared with the ineptness of the Scottish king's decisions, who himself received far less support than he could have expected from his 'new weapons' and French-inspired tactics, or conceivably could have hoped for from his Borderers and Highlanders. Unlike the reverses suffered in earlier forays, however, the defeat at Flodden would turn out to be irretrievable.

EPILOGUE

NO WAY BACK

Where shiver'd was fair Scotland's spear
And broken was her shield
                Sir Walter Scott, *Marmion*

WHATEVER THE TRUE significance of Flodden, the immediate reaction in Scotland to the defeat was to play down its effects and to demonstrate how far things would continue as before. At the same time there was both anger and disbelief at the result and some seeking of scapegoats. The returning soldiers entered a country not just in mourning but burningly resentful at the failure of Scottish arms. Their reception, however, was far more favourable than that of the army's French advisers who, before they could reach the Scottish east coast and take ships for France, were cut to pieces by the 'vengeful local people.'[1]

Together with such rage came incredulity both at the immense risks their king had taken and at the horrendous scale of the casualties, especially among the country's leaders. In answer to the call Andrew Pitcairn took his seven sons to battle: all were killed. His widow was pregnant and subsequently delivered a posthumous son to carry on the family line. However, such was the attitude to the defeated army that she and her infant son were initially turned off the Pitcairn estate until King James V interceded on their behalf.[2]

Among the survivors was a weaver called Fletcher, the sole representative of an eighty-man contingent sent to the muster by the small township of Selkirk in the Scottish Borders. During the battle he fought against the English vanguard and captured the flag of Sir Christopher Savage of Macclesfield. Legend has it that on his return he was so overcome with emotion – and guilt over his own survival – that he could not speak but instead dipped the flag in tribute to his lost comrades. This made such an impression that his gesture is re-enacted each year in prolonged ceremonies climaxed by 'a casting of the colours' in Selkirk's market place.

In Scotland today observances of the great battle are restricted to the border towns and to the field itself, although some memories are kept alive through local folklore. Few survivors, for instance, returned to Caithness in the far north. Consequently, it has long been considered unlucky for anyone leaving that shire to wear green, the colour of the doublets worn by those who accompanied their earl to the Flodden muster.[3]

Given the circumstances it is unsurprising there were no contemporary descriptions of the battle from a Scottish point of view and that Scottish records for the period are also so scarce. Historian Michael Brander in his study of border ballads has concluded that there were, in fact, no contemporary ones on Flodden, although today Flodden is closely linked with the widely recognised lament *The Flowers of the Forest*.[4] For many years this was thought to be a genuine Scottish song of the period until Sir Walter Scott discovered it had been written in the mid-eighteenth century by Miss Jane Elliot, daughter of Sir Gilbert Elliot, Lord Chief Justice Clerk of Scotland, and based on an earlier song written by Mrs Patrick Cockburn of Ormiston – which, in its turn, was apparently written some considerable time after the battle. This, of course, in no way prevents Miss Elliot's song from being an undoubted masterpiece: apart from its haunting melody she genuinely succeeds in catching the sense of loss, not just for the dead but for the seemingly golden age under James IV that had gone forever.

> The flowers of the forest, that faught aye the foremost
> The prime o' our land now lie cauld in the clay
> ... We'll hear nae mair littin' at our ewe-milkin',

Women and bairns are dowie and wae,
Sighin' and moanin' on ilka green loanin,
The flowers of the forest are a' wede away.[5]

It was not until the early nineteenth century that Sir Walter Scott wrote his own epic poem, *Marmion*, an unashamed romance of unrequited love with Flodden providing the powerful backdrop. But memorable as many of its lines might be they draw on Victorian notions of chivalry and conduct and make no serious attempt to describe the course of the battle faithfully.[6]

The dearth of contemporary material indicates that in Scotland immediately after Flodden there was a resolve either not to mention the battle or even in certain cases to ignore the result by circulating reports of James' survival. The patriotic Scottish historian, John Lesley, writing around 1570, even stated baldly that 'although many Englishmen were slain many alleged that we lost the field'.[7]

There were, of course, far better reasons for minimising the result than those of embarrassment or disbelief: the English were expected to mount a counter invasion and time could be far better spent in preparation than in lamentations. When Edinburgh received news of the disaster the day after the battle, the city fully anticipated becoming the target for a rampaging English army. Although the city's Provost and his deputy were among those killed at Flodden, the town council instantly ordered all citizens fit to bear arms to assemble in array at the jowing (tolling) of the common bell; women were told not to be found clamouring and crying in the street but rather repairing to the churches to offer up prayers for success.

The council's next objective was to extend the city's fortifications. The Grass market and Cow market were then outside the protection of the city's walls. A considerable extension to the wall was therefore undertaken at the south-east corner of the Castle rock, from where it descended obliquely to the West

Port before rising again towards the High Riggs on the line of a steep lane called the Vennel and, finally, turning eastward to run along the north side of the garden of Heriot's hospital. Although constructed in great haste, using mass citizen labour, it was well-built and erected, complete with gun ports, using slabs of red sandstone quarried nearby. Although most of it has been demolished for subsequent development, the sections still standing along the north side of Heriot's hospital garden and in Cowgate compare well with a further extension built in 1620.[8]

Defensive measures were not limited to Edinburgh. Ten days after Flodden the nation's lords met in Council and decided to call in all available weapons and other materials of war. At the same time they approved the rapid coronation of a new king – just seventeen months old – which took place on 21 September. In the meantime, a Council of Regency was appointed to work with the Queen Mother in guarding the affairs of the nation but, there being far from universal confidence in a sister of Henry VIII having such responsibility, an invitation was subsequently sent to France to John, Duke of Albany, for him to become governor and heir to the throne in the event of both the young sovereign and his infant brother dying. In such ways determined attempts were made in Scotland to put Flodden behind them.

For quite different reasons the battle was given inadequate recognition in England. After Henry was sent news of it by Catherine, his queen, who emphasised the victory by enclosing a portion of James' blood-stained cloak – the king duly ordered his cannon to be fired in celebration and a Te Deum high mass to be sung in the captured French city of Tournai. In reality Henry's easily aroused jealousy was very likely to have been stirred by Surrey's success, particularly compared with the king's over-praised tactical success at the Battle of the Spurs, in which he was not personally involved. The niggardliness of Henry's awards to the victorious commanders at Flodden were testimony to such feelings.[9] Henry's frustration was probably increased when bad weather rather than any directives he gave to his navy led to the grounding of James IV's immensely expensive toy, his flagship the *St Michael* (which was eventually sold to France for much less than it had cost to build).

The Scots, however, deceived themselves in anticipating an early English invasion. The English under Surrey did not even have the chance to carouse over their victory and it was only in later years that ballads were commissioned – by non-Howard commanders – to celebrate their triumph there. In any case it had never been Surrey's intention to push deep into Scotland; indeed he lacked the logistic means, the numbers and the authority of Henry VIII to do so. On 14 September he disbanded his troops, justifying such swift action, and such marked lack of gratitude to those who had served him so well, by declaring that he had spared the Exchequer 'the wages of 18,689 men for a fortnight'.[10] Similarly with a callousness and marked lack of charity, Surrey had his force collect the bodies of those killed in the battle and bury the majority in common graves near to where they fell, some being close-packed in a 'hole hastily dug' within the churchyard of the small church at Branxton.[11]

The manner and speed of the mass interments which, of course, took place on English soil, gave their opponents little or no opportunity to remove their slain leaders or to conduct any appropriate ceremonies over them. In fact, it has been suggested that the tomb to John, Lord Semple, in the remains of the Collegiate church at Castle Semple was probably the only contemporary memorial to such Scottish leaders.[12]

The lack of acclaim and proper dignity for the Scottish casualties at Flodden was to be equalled by the treatment of their king. Following his identification on the morning after the battle his body was embalmed, encased in lead and, despite Bishop Ruthall's desire for Durham to have such a powerful trophy, sent down to London in a closed cart. The body was taken to the Carthusian monastery of Sheen, seven miles from London where, as an ex-communicate, it remained unburied. Henry VIII subsequently requested permission from Pope Leo X to bury the corpse and had apparently designed an appropriate funeral in which he would play a prominent role himself. Any such permission would need to work on the assumption that James would have shown some signs of repentance during his death throes, if not before.[13] However, by the time it was received Henry had lost interest and the body remained unburied for many years until the religious house was dissolved and became the home of the Duke of Suffolk. There the antiquary John Stowe was shown the body, from which some workmen had apparently hewed the head 'for their foolish pleasure', and Stowe saw both portions lying in a waste room amid other rubble.[14] Subsequently Launcelot Young, master glazier to Elizabeth I, taken by the sweet odour coming from the embalmed head (complete with its red hair and beard) carried it to his London home in Wood Street where he kept it as a grisly pot pourri. He finally had the sexton of his local church of St Michael's bury it amongst other bones from their charnel, at which point any further record was lost.

In spite of the attempts on both sides to put Flodden behind them, its significance soon became apparent. Henry VIII's cavalier disregard for James IV's body not only showed a lack of chivalry towards his enemy, but also demonstrated his conviction that he could act with impunity now that Scotland no longer represented a serious military threat. In any case, he came to realise that he had been duped into war with France by his Spanish father-in-law and his new priority now was to make a truce with France prior to opening peace negotiations. These also revealed Scotland's reduced position for, although the country was included in the subsequent agreement, France, for whom so many sacrifices had been made, did not even consult its traditional ally and Scotland's inclusion was only on the express condition that if any sizeable raids were mounted against England its provisions would no longer apply. To compound France's shabby treatment of the Scots, Louis XII also delayed Albany's move back from France.

Such actions reflected the changed pattern of power for, during the next ninety years until England and Scotland came to share the same (Scottish) monarch, the northern kingdom never remotely regained the level of internal cohesion nor the confidence it had enjoyed when James IV led the Scottish host into England. Henry, therefore, could continue his clumsy attempts to move in the mainstream of European politics until, learning from his mistakes, he eventually became as adept a player as any of his contemporaries. Meanwhile, France came to realise that henceforth Scotland could not be expected to adopt any offensive strategy against England without major military assistance.[15] In fact, under its boy king a new instability so beset the country that people only travelled 'through the countryside in large companies all armed with pikes, swords and bucklers and a half pike in their hands'.[16]

Among the rival factions were Anglophiles and Francophiles and, before James V eventually assumed power in 1528, the powerful Douglas family moved the Anglophiles into the ascendant. Although James V subsequently succeeded in crushing the Douglases, other Scottish magnates, whether influenced by offers of English gold or not, came to feel their future lay with the 'auld enemy' and from the 1530s onward, with the spread of the Reformation to Scotland, this trend grew. Even those not so disposed tended to be more cautious in supporting military initiatives against England. In 1523, for instance, when England and France were at war and France sent over a contingent to support a possible invasion of England, the Scottish magnates accompanying the force refused to cross the border. They would again refuse to do so in the early part of 1542, 1545 and finally in 1557.

However, immediately after the battle the true extent of Scottish military weakness was yet to become clear. While aggressive moves southward were far more unlikely, when Henry VIII attempted to escalate destructive English raids across the border he quickly met Scotland's long-renowned resilience in defence, and failed to gain the successes he anticipated. Scotland's fighting men, in this case the Borderers, appeared as formidable as ever and over the next 30 years the country would show itself capable of seeing off English raiders, with successes at Hadden Rigg in 1542 against some 3000 English soldiers and at Ancrum Moor in 1545 against a force close to 5000 men. However, the continuing internal divisions and relatively limited resources allocated for military purposes made it impossible to keep fully abreast with military developments elsewhere in Europe, and as a result, attempts to use the Scottish host against major English incursions proved disastrous.

James V – seeking as all kings must to establish his royal supremacy – lost many of his best and foremost fighters, notably the Douglases, and he paid a terrible penalty for the reputation he acquired of always taking rather than giving from his nobility.[17] After assembling a large army in 1542 to repel troops sent by Henry VIII in a renewal of his claims to suzerainty over Scotland, James was taken ill and it was left to his subordinate commanders to supervise the 18,000-man force as it burnt households and drove off cattle just south of the border. Lord Robert Maxwell, Oliver Sinclair and others became aware of an English force apparently boxing them in between a bog and the River Esk and were faced by attacks from a small number of Border horse led by Thomas Barton, captain of Carlisle Castle. After sustaining just twenty casualties, the Scots panicked in a way never before seen in the history of Scottish arms and the army was destroyed. To break in face of a much weaker force was a tragedy caused primarily by weak and disunited leadership. In the process the English acquired many influential prisoners, but more disastrous still, Scotland lost another king who, already much diminished by illness, reacted to the news so badly that he was dead within three months.

Five years later, another major clash ended in scarcely more fortunate circumstances, this time primarily due to deficiencies in the Scottish supporting arms. Following Henry's death, Edward Seymour, Duke of Somerset, who took on the title of Lord Protector of England during King Edward VI's minority, continued English attempts to force Scotland into accepting a marriage between their young queen, Mary, and Edward VI. Somerset's strategy was not only to invade Scotland but to establish a permanent garrison there as well, which brought about a clash between his army of 17,000 men (including 3000 mercenaries) and 23,000 or more Scots under their regent, James Hamilton, Earl of Arran. This took place at Pinkie, near Musselburgh, and ended in outright victory for the well-balanced and well-led English force, with its infantry backed by heavy cavalry and copious artillery, including supporting fire from English ships lying just off shore. Once more Scottish soldiers fought with amazing bravery – although the Highlanders panicked after being fired on by artillery – but the feudal host proved no match for the better-equipped English army. As in the past, however, winning set battles without being able to dominate the whole of the country produced an inconclusive result and in 1550, after the English were defeated in France, they agreed to withdraw their troops from Scotland. Their aim of bringing about the union of the two countries had again foundered.

For Scotland, however, there was no escaping the consequences of Flodden; subsequent military weakness left them dangerously vulnerable, this time to their erstwhile ally, France. In 1558, after the marriage of Mary, Queen of Scots, to Francis, the French dauphin, the country seemed likely to become the equivalent of a French province. Such a prospect caused a group of Scottish magnates calling themselves the Lords of the Congregation to attack both the Scottish Catholic church and the French alliance. In a remarkable volte-face these new patriots saw France, rather than England, as their deadly enemy – but they lacked the means to attack the French military units garrisoned in Scotland. They turned for help to the adjoining

Protestant nation that shared the same island, spoke the same language and had an age-old antipathy to France.

Elizabeth I was Queen of England and together with her astute minister, Cecil, she viewed the likely defeat of the Scottish Protestants, and with it the confirmation of Scotland as a satellite of Catholic France, as a serious threat both to the English Reformation and to England's security. In 1560, therefore, at Berwick, a treaty was made with the Scottish Protestants to safeguard the 'freedom of the Crown of Scotland from conquest'. The English navy blocked the Forth and the French forces, now deprived of supplies, agreed to open negotiations, which resulted in a treaty, concluded in Edinburgh during July 1560, by which both the French and English agreed to leave Scotland. This spelt the end of both the 'auld alliance', cherished by Scotland since the time of William Wallace, and French domination of the country. In the long run, it left the way clear for King James VI of Scotland, after not protesting overmuch about the execution of his mother, Mary, in 1587, to become James I of England in 1603.

Flodden, therefore, turned out to be even more significant for the future of Scotland than the great victory gained by Robert Bruce over the English at Bannockburn that spear-headed the country's move towards renewed independence. The crushing nature of the defeat at Flodden, together with the subsequent military weakness and political upheavals after the death of James IV, heralded a confused period in the nation's history which culminated in the union of the Scottish and English crowns and, a century later, in the loss of Scottish independence through political union.

At Branxton on 9 September 2001, the author attended a service of commemoration on Piper's Hill for those who fell in the battle waged there 488 years before. The party, led by a priest whose robes flapped madly in the wind, included a piper, standard bearers, clan representatives and a handful of committed spectators. By the memorial cross a service was held 'for the brave men who fell on both sides'. This included a short address and two minutes silence, followed by the ineffably mournful piping of the 'Flowers of the Forest' and the laying of wreaths. Afterwards I watched the procession descend the hill and begin making its way along the road to Branxton church. Above the moaning of the wind came snatches of 'Scotland the Brave' and I was filled with wonder at such a service of tribute for those past warriors – some of whom I had come to know so well – together with a sense of privilege at having shared in it. This, however, was soon followed by my conviction that, in spite of such a commemoration, those who fought so tenaciously at Branxton and died in their thousands there have received scant recognition. Some reasons are fully understandable, including a proud country's anger and shame at the defeat, an English king's reluctance to give the battle precedence over the relatively minor clashes of his French campaign, the determination of the English commander at Flodden not to stand accused of exaggerating his success and, in the case of England, because other martial successes, such as Pinkie, would soon follow it.

This, however, is far from the whole story. In Scotland there has been continuing ambivalence over the battle's long-term effects, mostly arising from difficulties in squaring the fact that their very competent king could decide to invade England for no good reasons of state and before he had fully united his country behind him. Such puzzlement has been linked with a sense of betrayal associated with a battle that, because of Scotland's famed martial qualities and because of the perceived, if mistaken, superiority of their army of the day, its soldiers should surely have won. Never mind the protracted uncertainty before the final outcome, nor the remarkable performance of the English, Flodden has tended to be downplayed to the present day.

This attitude was illustrated in 1943 when General Douglas Wimberley, commander of 51 Highland division under Field-Marshal Montgomery, was saying goodbye to his men. As a commander he was well known for emphasising his formation's distinctly Scottish nature and the influence of past deeds upon its performance. Within his farewell Order of the Day he quoted a verse from the Scottish press that had been written for his division and emphasising the strength of Scottish military traditions:

Ye canna mak' a sujer wi' braid an trappin's braw,
Nor gie him fightin' spirit when his back's agin the wa',
It's the breedin' in the vallants that wanna let them whine,
The bluid o' generations frae lang, lang syne.

For Wimberley this fighting tradition was built both before and after union. It was seen 'at Bannockburn, Culloden, Waterloo, the Alma and at Loos'.[18] Significantly, he made no mention of Flodden, a battle of far more significance than the Jacobites' defeat in their last doomed – and uncoordinated – charge at Culloden.

In other circles the sentiments associated with the battle seem to be more of anger than betrayal. With the killing of the king at Flodden the hopes he embodied of a Celtic state also died. There remains the beguiling picture of another Scotland prior to what Raymond Campbell Paterson, falsely but revealingly, calls 'the long sleep of union'.[19] Before Flodden a proud, if still backward and savage, country under its Stewart kings appeared to be developing quickly according to its Celtic traditions until, through a combination of defeat and the coming of the Reformation – a link recognised by one writer who described Flodden as the reveille of the Reformation for Scotland[20] – it was driven into the arms of its traditional enemy.

For strong Celtic nationalists no matter the release of energy previously committed to internal feuding which resulted in the Scottish Enlightenment with its towering figures of David Hume, one of the greatest philosophers in the English language, Adam Smith, the father of economics, and literary giants such as Robert Burns and Sir Walter Scott. No matter the country's immense achievements in heavy and civil engineering, in manufacturing, in sociology and architecture, in geology and science, in medicine and statistics, in theology and mathematics, in law and banking, in shipping and other forms of transportation, in exploration and missionary work, in education and town planning, in the development of television and penicillin, and in dominating British parliaments.

For such as them, Celtic Scotland, a model all the more alluring for not having had to tack its way through the political and economic gales of the last 500 years, should never be fully at home with union, nor probably for that matter with a devolved Scotland within the union, and they can never forget that Flodden opened the gates for such assimilation.

The majority of Scots, in spite of understandable regrets that their soldiers failed to beat the English more often, are surely closer in thought to such writers as Professor Tom Divine, who believes that union did not dilute the sense of Scottish identity but strengthened it by powerfully reinforcing their sense of national esteem.[21]

Surely the time has come for the great battle fought amid the bleak Northumberland hills half a millennium ago to be recognised in both countries for what it was, a highly influential and heroic action within the catalogue of military engagements between them. Fought on the English side of the border it is perhaps optimistic to expect Scots to commemorate it in anything like the numbers who flock to the mournful site of Culloden Moor, despite the fact that Flodden involved the whole Scottish host and most of the country's nobility under a Stewart king who had already enjoyed a distinguished reign of twenty-five years, compared with the undoubtedly gallant, if near hopeless and short-lived, action by a comparatively small and heterogeneous force led by an exiled Stewart prince.

Culloden was a desperate and doomed last stand, but despite the poignancy which clings to the Jacobites' defeat, a deeper, rawer nerve is touched by Flodden. It was, finally, an ignominious, disastrous defeat for the Scots, and it stands in the history of the nation as its most significant battlefield encounter.

APPENDIX

≈

EXPLORING THE FLODDEN BATTLEFIELD

THE DIRECTIONS WHICH follow should be used in conjunction with Ordnance Survey Explorer Map 339, scale 1:25000, covering Kelso, Coldstream and the Lower Tweed Valley. They involve both walking and driving, especially if one intends to follow the armies' approach marches.

However, anyone interested in visiting the battlefield itself should start at the village of Branxton (grid reference 894 377). From Branxton your first move should be to the memorial on its little eminence of Piper's Hill. From the village follow the minor road westward where, after 100 metres, you will see Branxton church on your right-hand side. Following the battle this was used as a mortuary.

The memorial car park is a further 500 metres on your left. From there wooden steps (complete with balustrade) lead up to the large commemorative cross. At its southernmost edge a viewscape carries a diagram of both sides' formations and battle positions. From this you will realise you are at the point where the Admiral, Surrey's eldest son and English vanguard commander, faced attack from the Scottish division commanded by Errol, Crawford and Montrose. Ahead and above is the crest of Branxton Hill that was occupied by the Scottish battle lines. Their earlier position on Flodden Hill is some three kilometres to the south and east, screened from view by Branxton Hill. Note how the ground quickly falls away immediately in front of you. At its low point a stream runs from left to right, before the slopes rise towards the crest of Branxton Hill. To the right the ground is considerably more even; this was the line of approach of the division commanded by Home and Huntly when they attacked the formations on the English right flank commanded by Edmund Howard. Along the ridge to your left the principal Scottish division under King James IV attacked the English rearguard, commanded by the Earl of Surrey. In fact, after repelling their own attackers, the Admiral's forces were able to move across from their station here on Piper's Hill to assist his father.

To your far left is Pace Hill (GR 915 375) occupied by the Scottish Highlanders under Argyll and Lennox. You can make out this hill by the wooded plantations on its northern and western slopes. The Highlanders were subsequently surprised by the English division under Stanley who ascended Pace Hill from its eastern flank.

By comparing the formations shown on the viewscape with the battle maps in this book and, when necessary, checking both out against its analysis of the conflict, you should not only be able to follow the sequence of the Scottish attacks upon Branxton ridge, but the subsequent course of the battle as well.

Visitors who are short of time could well conclude that such an appreciation is sufficient. However, for further information on the battle, head for Etal Castle (GR 928 393), six kilometres away, where there are panoramic bays depicting the conflict, the combatants and the weapons used.

Visitors with considerably more time can, if they so wish, follow the approach marches undertaken by both armies and thereby understand further the major role played by the ground in the final outcome. Those intending to follow the whole of the suggested course face a combination of driving and walking requiring a full day. However, some optional short-cuts are offered and, because visitors might have particular allegiances, the route taken by each army will be considered separately.

The Scottish Army's Trail

James IV's offensive began with his crossing the Tweed. His first major obstacle on the river's southern side was Norham Castle, which he seized after smashing down its defences with his heavy artillery. Norham, therefore, is a convenient point to join the Scottish army in its move towards battle. To get there from the Flodden memorial it is suggested you drive from Branxton to Crookham and then take the A69 westwards to Cornhill (six kilometres) before proceeding northwards along the A698 for eight kilometres until you reach the Salutation Inn (GR 924 467), where you turn west to Norham 2.5 kilometres away. The castle is administered by Scottish Heritage and a guide book on Norham is available. This contains an account of James IV's attack.

From Norham you can closely follow the subsequent progress of the Scottish army. Move along the B6470 in an easterly direction for some seven kilometres to the junction with the B6354. Turn right here and head south for 8.5 kilometres past Duddo village (whose castle James also destroyed) until you reach Etal Castle. This provides a good example of one of the smaller border fortifications taken by James IV during his progress south. As mentioned earlier it also contains a series of bays depicting the Battle of Flodden, including the soldiers' weapons and equipment.

From Etal continue on the B6354 to a point just north of Ford Castle – where James spent time with Lady Heron before the battle. It is not suggested you visit the castle, it is now a private study centre, but turn right and drive along the B6354 for 1700 metres to a T-junction where you again turn right, this time along the A697, for 500 metres. At Fisher's Steads turn left along a minor road; after 1200 metres you will reach a small row of dwellings at Blinkbonny (GR 909 364). Leave your car here and take the footpath up Flodden Hill, where the Scottish army set up its fortified camp prior to moving across to Branxton. From the top of Flodden Hill you can assess the remarkable strength of the defensive position chosen by the Scottish king, particularly against an English army coming northwards from Milfield. To the north-west is the shallow saddle leading to Branxton Hill some 2.5 kilometres away across which James subsequently led his army, complete with its heavy guns.

On returning to Blinkbonny continue westwards along the minor road for one kilometre before turning right along another minor road signposted to Branxton. After about 800 metres you can see on your left-hand side the positions occupied by the Scots on Branxton Hill. Leave your car at this point and, if you have binoculars, you should be able to make out the memorial cross marking the English position on Piper's Hill. Like James IV, you will see how this looks far less of an obstacle than it proved on the day of battle. The road descends sharply down Branxton Hill towards the ridge held by the English on 9 September 1513. At GR 896 372 the road crosses the small stream which gave the attacking Scots so many problems and contributed markedly to their destruction. By continuing into Branxton you have completed the journey taken by the Scottish army.

The English Army's Trail

When the English realised that Flodden Hill was virtually impregnable, they decided on two long approach marches, one on the day preceding the battle and the other on the actual day of battle. Initially, they marched eighteen kilometres or so from the neighbourhood of Wooler to make camp on Bar moor Ridge (GR 968 391) from where, on the following day, they planned to march westward for some ten kilometres before crossing the River Till, either at Twizel Bridge or at Castle Heaton, and then to move south for a final six kilometres to Branxton.

Those wishing to retrace the entire English march should drive from Branxton to Crookham and then move south along the A697 to Wooler (thirteen kilometres). From Wooler you can join the English route northwards via Doddington (GR 998 325) and then, by a succession of minor roads, follow it to Bar moor Ridge. This will help you to appreciate the significant length of the flank march (which due to the adverse weather experienced in 1513 would have been along muddy and flooded tracks), while at the same time deciding for yourselves whether or not the Scots would be capable of shelling the advancing English columns from their fortress on Flodden Hill. On arriving at Bar moor you can climb Watchlaw Hill (as the Admiral did on the night preceeding the battle) and if equipped with binoculars look across to Flodden Hill, which in poor weather will be exceedingly difficult to make out. Alternatively, you can drive directly from Branxton to Bar moor Wood (GR 968 391), where the English camped prior to commencing their second leg. The suggested route to Bar moor is via Crookham and Ford.

From Bar moor head north then west along minor roads to Duddo (GR 937 427). (Alternatively, you could take the simpler route to Duddo via the B6353 from Bar moor to Ford and then along the B6354.) At Duddo drive west for two kilometres to a road/track junction (GR 918 424). If you are energetic and wish to assess where the English rearguard were most likely to have forded the Till, park your car at the junction and walk straight ahead along the muddy, rutted track for some further two kilometres. On your arrival you can look down upon the river and note the probable crossing place to the south of Heaton Mill House. Here you can appreciate the steepness of the river banks which the English had to negotiate, together with the considerable width of the river itself. On returning to your car, continue west along the minor road for a further 3.5 kilometres to Twizel Bridge (GR 885 433) where the English vanguard, cavalry and artillery crossed the Till. From there drive westwards along the A698 for

800 metres before turning left (south) along a minor road towards Crookham. Whatever the balance of the detachments that crossed the Till either at Castle Heaton or Twizel, the English combined to move south into the Palinsburn valley. Here they were able to form up along the lower reaches of Branxton Hill where they could keep out of sight until they were ready to move onto the ridge – including Piper's Hill – to await the Scottish attack from Branxton summit. From Crookham follow the minor road along the Palinsburn valley to Branxton, where the trail ends.

However, while driving to Branxton, the more adventurous and well-shod might consider a final short walk. The object here would be to locate the Branx Brig across which so many of the English forces negotiated the flooded reaches of the Palinsburn valley. To do so, stop at a point some 1300 metres after leaving Crookham. Beside a farmhouse on the right-hand side there is a stile and sign indicating a footpath to Inch plantation. Cross the stile, then move along a muddy and little trodden footpath for 400 metres until it enters Inch plantation and brings you to the brig which, although much overgrown and neglected, still survives.

NOTES

PROLOGUE: BURGHMUIR – AUGUST 1513

1 Pitscottie, Robert Lindsay of *The Historie and Chronicles of Scotland*, ed. Aeneas J.G. Mackay, Edinburgh 1899–1922, 257–8
2 *Accounts of the Lord High Treasurer of Scotland*, ed. James Balfour Paul and T. Dickson, Edinburgh 1877–1916, vol iv, 416
3 Mackie, R.L. *King James IV of Scotland*, Edinburgh 1958, 247
4 Smith, Charles J. *Historic South Edinburgh*, Edinburgh 2000, 2
5 Scott, Sir Walter *Poetical Works*, London 1869, 95
6 *Treasurer's* Accounts, *op cit*, vol iv, 521
7 Pitscottie, *Historie*, *op cit*, 261
8 Buchanan, George *History of Scotland*, transl. James Aitkin, Glasgow 1827, 250
9 Pitscottie, *Historie*, *op cit*, 258–9
10 Mackie, *King James IV*, *op cit*, 243–4

CHAPTER ONE: THE DEFENDERS

1 Nicholson, Ranald *Scotland: The Later Middle Ages*, Edinburgh 1989, 23
2 Smith, T.B. *A Short Commentary on the Law of Scotland*, Edinburgh 1962, 16
3 Poole, A.L. *Domesday Book to Magna Carta 1087–1216*, Oxford, 1987, 287
4 'Honour' was the title given to the sum of the lands forming a barony
5 Stevenson, J. *Documents Illustrative of the History of Scotland*, 1870, vol i, 36ff
6 Barrow, G.W.S. *Robert Bruce and the Community of Scotland*, Edinburgh 1996, 177

7 Hyland, Ann *The Warhorse*, Sutton 1998, 31

8 By 1330 Henry Percy had recovered his Scottish lands, but the others, including the most prominent such as Wake, Zouche and Beaumont, remained disappointed

9 Capgrave, John *The Book of the Illustrious Henries*, ed. F. Hingeston, 1858

10 Historically, a librate was a piece of land worth a pound a year

11 Nicholson, Ranald, *Scotland, op cit*, 129

12 Fordun, John of *Chronicles of the Scottish Nation*, ed. W.F. Skene 187, 217–8, 224, 227–31

13 Edward III expended £16,000 in 1336 alone. Nicolson, Ranald, *Scotland, op cit*, 135

14 Grant, Alexander *Independence and Nationhood, Scotland 1306–1469*, Edinburgh 2001, 31

15 Bower, Walter *Scoticronicon*, ed. D. E. R. Watt, 1987, book viii

16 *Ibid*, book xvi, ch 30, 17, 23–5

17 *Ibid*, book xvi, ch 35, 127–35

18 Brown, Michael *James I*, Edinburgh 1994, 203

19 *Ibid*, 114–5

20 *Ibid*, 116

21 McGladdery, Christine *James II*, Edinburgh 1990, 54–5

22 *Ibid*, 155; *Exchequer Rolls of Scotland*, ed. Stuart and Burnett, Edinburgh 1878–1908, vol vi, 383

23 Major, John *A History of Greater Britain*, Edinburgh 1892, 385

24 *Acts of the Parliaments of Scotland*, ed. T. Thomson and C. Innes, Edinburgh 1814–75, 18c 10–14; 23c 17

25 Stevenson, J. *Letters and Papers Illustrative of the Wars of the English in France*, 1861, vol i, 319–20

26 *Rotuli Scotiae in Turri Londinensi et in Domo Capitulari West-monasteriensi Asservati*, ed. D. Macpherson 1814–19, vol ii, 360–1

27 MacDougall, Norman *James III, A Political Study*, Edinburgh 1982, 42–3

28 McGladdery, Christine, *James II, op cit*, 156

29 *The Auchinleck Chronicle*, f.119v

30 MacDougall, Norman *James IV* East Linton 1997, iii

31 *Acts of the Parliaments of Scotland, op cit*, 186

32 *Treasurer's Accounts, op cit*, vol i, 49

33 MacDougall, Norman *James III, op cit*, 306; *Treasurer's Accounts*, vol i, 54, 66, 68

34 *Ibid*, 299

35 Lesley, John *The History of Scotland from the Death of King James I to the year* 1561, Bannatyne Club 1830, 43
36 MacDougall, Norman *James III, op cit*, 154–5
37 Scarisbrick, J.J. *Henry VIII*, Eyre Methuen 1976, 653

CHAPTER TWO: PROUD MONARCHS

1 Chrimes, S.B. *Henry VII*, 1972, 276
2 Buchanan, George *History of Scotland, op cit*, 261
3 *Treasurer's Accounts, op cit*, vol i, 95
4 *Exchequer Rolls of Scotland, op cit*, vol xii, 181
5 *Calendar of State Papers*, Spain, vol i, no 210
6 Mackie, R.L. *King James IV of Scotland, op cit*, 201
7 *Treasurer's Accounts, op cit*, vol i, 267
8 *Exchequer Rolls of Scotland, op cit*, vol xii, x/ix
9 *Treasurer's Accounts, op cit*, vol i, 195–7
10 *Treasurer's Accounts, ibid*, vol i, 313–3
11 MacDougall, Norman *James IV, op cit*, 1997, 133–4
12 *Treasurer's Accounts, op cit*, vol i, 313–4
13 *Calendar of Documents Relating to Scotland*, ed J. Bain, 1881–8, vol iv, no 1644
14 Gairdner, James *Henry VII*, London 1889, 180–3
15 MacDougall, Norman *James IV, op cit*, 223; James IV Letters no 42
16 *Exchequer Rolls of Scotland, op cit*, vol xii, xxxv
17 Richmond, C.F. 'English Naval Power in the Fifteenth Century', *History*, Feb 1967, vol ii, no 174, 6–7
18 Mackie, J.D. *The Earlier Tudors 1485–1558*, Oxford 1988, 211–12
19 Mackie, R.L. *James IV, op cit*, 63; Pitscottie, *Historie, op cit*, vol i, 226–7
20 *Treasurer's Accounts, op cit*, vol i, 120
21 *Treasurer's Accounts, op cit*, vol iv, 451–507
22 Scarisbrick, J.J. *Henry VII, op cit*, 33
23 Scarisbrick, J.J. *ibid*, 38
24 Pollard, A.F. *Henry VIII*, London 1902, 36, 37
25 Mackie, J.D. *The Earlier Tudors, op cit*, 268
26 Scarisbrick, J.J. *Henry VII, op cit*, 33

CHAPTER THREE: SLIDE TOWARDS WAR

1 Mackie, J.D. *The Earlier Tudors, op cit*, 159

2 Mackie, R.L. *Transactions of the Franco-Scottish Society 1919–1935*, vol viii 37–56

3 Gat, Azar *A History of Military Thought*, Oxford 2001, 4–11

4 *Letters and Papers of Henry VIII, Foreign and Domestic 1509–47*, vol i, 5(ii)

5 *Supplement to the State Papers Spanish and Bergenroth*; Pollard, A.F. *Henry VIII*, 1902, 39

6 Scarisbrick, J. J. *Henry VIII, op cit*, 40, 41

7 *Diplomatic Correspondence between the Courts of France and Scotland 1507–1517*, *(Flodden Papers)* ed. Marguerite Wood, Edinburgh 1933, xxiv–xxxiii

8 *Letters and Papers of Henry VIII, op cit*, vol i, 1690

9 *Epistolae Regum Scotorum*, 1722 vol i, 122

10 *Letters of James IV 1505–1513*, ed. R.L. Mackie, Edinburgh 1953, no 543

11 *Diplomatic Correspondence, op cit*, xvii

12 *Ibid*, 79–83

13 Burton, John Hill *The History of Scotland*, William Blackwood 1897, vol ii, 73

14 *Letters of James IV, op cit*, no 550

15 Barr, Niall *Flodden 1513*, Stroud 2001, 30

16 *Letters of James IV, op cit*, no 563

CHAPTER FOUR: THE SOLDIERS AND THEIR WEAPONS

1 Scarisbrick, J.J. *Henry VIII, op cit*, 57

2 Oman, Sir Charles *A History of the Art of War in the 16th Century*, Greenhill Books, 1987, 290

3 *Letters and Papers of Henry VIII, op cit*, vol i, 631, no 4306

4 Rymer, Thomas *Foeder Conventiones Literae*, The Hague 1739–45, 3rd edn, xii, 355

5 Cornish Paul and McBride, Angus *Henry VIII's Army*, Osprey 2000, 22

6 Scarisbrick, J.J. *Henry VIII, op cit*, 57

7 Mackie R.L. *Transactions of the Franco-Scottish Society, op cit*, vol viii, 60–69

8 Toughened brass was comparable to modern gun metal or bronze

9 *Letters and Papers of Henry VIII, op cit*, vol i, no 2651

10 Blackmore, H.L. *The Armouries of the Tower of London*, HMSO 1976, 108

11 Hogg, O.F. *English Artillery 1326–1716*, 1963, 213–5

12 This figure was arrived at by Colonel H.C.B. Rogers in his book

Artillery through the Ages and cited by Colonel A. Guinan in a paper he sent to the author on 17 December 2002

13 Hogg, *English Artillery, op cit*, 214–5

14 Hall, E. *The Triumphant Reigne of Kyng Henry VIII*, London 1904, 555

15 *Calendar of State Papers, Venice, 1509–1519*, vol i, London 1867, 316

16 Mackenzie, W.M. *The Secret of Flodden*, Edinburgh 1931, 71

17 McCormack, John *One Million Mercenaries, Swiss Soldiers in the Armies of the World*, 1993, iii

18 Hall, E., *Triumphant Reigne, op cit* anno v, folio xxxvii

19 *The English Army at Flodden*, ed. J.D. Mackie, 1951, vol 8 57

CHAPTER FIVE: THE ENGLISH COMMANDERS

1 Campbell, W. *Materials for a History of the Reign of Henry VII*, 1877, ii, 480

2 Weir, Alison *Henry VIII King and Court*, 2001, 105

3 MacDougall, Norman *James IV, op cit*, 139; Mackie, R.L. *James IV, op cit*, 87–8

4 Leland, John *De Rebus Britannicus Collectanea*, 1770, iv, 266

5 *Letters and Papers of Henry VII, op cit*, vol i, 444

6 Brewer, J.S. *The Reign of Henry VIII*, London 1884, vol i, no 3443

7 *Venetian Calendar*, iv, 294–5

8 Williamson, James A. *The Tudor Age*, 1958, 1126

9 Weever, John *Ancient Funeral Monuments*, Amsterdam 1979 838

10 Vokes, Susan Elisabeth, *PhD Thesis on the early career of Thomas Howard* Hull, 1988, 104

11 Smith, Lacey B. *A Tudor Tragedy: the Life and Times of Catherine Howard*, 1961, 27

12 *The Battle of Flodden Field*, ed. Weber, 37–40, 50–9

13 Brodie, Robert Henry *Sir Marmaduke Constable*, DNB 1995, 1

14 *Ballad of Flodden Field*, poem

15 *An Historical and Architectural Description of the Priory Church of Bridlington*, Cambridge, 1835, 194–7

16 *The Complete Peerage*, ed. by Vicary Gibbs, 1916, vol iv, 20

CHAPTER SIX: THE SCOTTISH COMMANDERS

1 MacDougall, Norman *James IV, op cit*, 306

2 Taylor, James *The Great Historic Families of Scotland*, 1889, vol i, 371
3 *Ibid*, 4
4 *Ibid*, vol ii, 292
5 *Ibid*, vol ii, 296
6 Henderson, Thomas Finlayson *DNB OUR* 1995, Third Earl of Huntly, 1
7 Gregory, D. *The History of the Western Highlands and Isles of Scotland*, Glasgow 1881, 96–112
8 Taylor, *Great Families*, *op cit*, vol ii, 298
9 Reese, Peter *The Scottish Commander*, Edinburgh 1999, 50
10 Wood, John Philip *The Peerage of Scotland*, Edinburgh 1813, vol ii, 95
11 Henderson, *op cit*, 1
12 Taylor, *Great Families*, *op cit*, vol i, 229
13 Wood, *op cit*, vol i, 85
14 Wood, *op cit*, vol i, 96; Taylor, *Great Families*, *op cit*, vol i, 231
15 *The Scots Peerage*, ed. Sir James Balfour Paul, Edinburgh 1905, vol i, 335
16 Henderson, *op cit*, Archibald Campbell, second Earl of Argyll, 1
17 Wood, *The Peerage*, *op cit*, vol i, 223
18 *The Scots Peerage*, *op cit*, 225

CHAPTER SEVEN: OPENING MOVES

1 Mackie, J.D. *op cit*, 246
2 Hall, E. *Triumphant Reigne*, *op cit*, vol i, 555–6
3 Mackie, J.D., *op cit*, 248–9
4 Saunders, Andrew *Norham Castle*, English Heritage 1998, 27 and following site plan
5 Barr, Niall *Flodden*, *op cit*, 65
6 Tradition has it that, while fishing in the Tweed, near Coldstream, James IV fell into one of the deep pools. On being rescued, he vowed to build a church to the Virgin Mary. This beautiful church, made entirely of stone, was constructed during the early sixteenth century, prior to Flodden.
7 Saunders, Andrew, *Norham Castle*, *op cit*, 24
8 *Letters and Papers of Henry VIII*, *op cit*, vol i no 2279
9 *Ibid*, vol i, no 4406
10 Hall, E. *Triumphant Reigne*, *op cit*, 558

11 *Treasurer's Accounts, op cit,* vol iv, 522
12 Mackie, J.D., *op cit,* 250; *Edinburgh Records,* vol I, 143
13 *Calendar of State Papers, Venice, op cit,* vol ii, no 341
14 *Articles of Battle,* Ruthall's letter to Wolsey; *Letters and Papers of Henry VIII op cit,* vol ii, 1005 and 1021
15 Hall, E. *Triumphant Reigne, op cit,* 557
16 *Diplomatic Correspondence, op cit,* x/iii
17 Hall, E. *Triumphant Reigne, op cit,* 557
18 *The Trewe Encountre,* London 1513, 145

CHAPTER EIGHT: JOCKEYING FOR POSITION

1 Hall, E. *Triumphant Reigne, op cit,* 558
2 *Ibid,* 559
3 *Trewe Encountre, op, cit,* 143
4 *Ibid,* 146
5 Barr, Niall, *Flodden, op cit,* 75
6 Hall, E. *Triumphant Reigne, op cit,* 560
7 *Trewe Encountre, op cit,* 146
8 *Ibid,* 146–7
9 Hall, E. *Triumphant Reigne, op cit,* 561
10 *Ibid,* 268

CHAPTER NINE: THE GUNS SPEAK

1 Hall, E. *Triumphant Reigne, op cit,* 561
2 *Ibid,* 561
3 *Letters and Papers of Henry VIII, op cit,* vol i, pt II, no 2283
4 Hall, E. *Triumphant Reigne, op cit,* 269
5 Barr, Niall *Flodden, op cit,* 81; Bergenroth, *Calendar of Letters, Spain, op cit,* vol i, no 210
6 Polydore, Vergil *The Anglica Historia,* ed. Denys Hays, RHS 1950, book xxv, 219
7 *Articles of Battle,* Account of the Battle of Flodden in Facsimiles of National Manuscripts by Sir Henry James, Part 2, Southampton 1865, 2

CHAPTER TEN: RIDING THE STORM

1 *Articles of Battle, op cit,* 2

2 Hall, E. *Triumphant Reigne, op cit,* 561
3 *Trewe Encountre, op cit,* 148
4 *Ibid,* 148
5 *Articles of Battle, op cit,* 2
6 Pitscottie, *Historie, op cit* 270
7 Leslie, John *The Historie of Scotland, op cit,* 94–5
8 Hall, E. *Triumphant Reigne, op cit,* 561
9 Barr, Niall, *Flodden, op cit,* 93; Caldwell, David H. *Scottish Weapons and Fortifications 1100–1800,* Edinburgh 1981, 77
10 Hall, E. *Triumphant Reigne, op cit,* 561

CHAPTER ELEVEN: FIGHT TO THE DEATH

1 *Articles of Battle, op cit,* 2
2 Kightly, Charles *Flodden: the Anglo-Scottish War of 1513,* 197 42
3 Hall, E. *Triumphant Reigne, op cit,* 562
4 Pitscottie, *Historie, op cit,* 271
5 Barr, Niall, *Flodden, op cit,* 105
6 Pitscottie, *Historie, op cit,* 271–2
7 *Articles of Battle, op cit,* 2
8 Kightly, Charles *Flodden, op cit,* 45
9 Hall, E. *Triumphant Reigne, op cit,* 562; *Articles of Battle, op cit,* 2
10 *Trewe Encountre, op cit,* 148
11 Baird, Ian F. (ed), *Scotish Feilde and Flodden Feilde, Two Flodden Poems,* 1982, 46
12 Kightly, Charles, *Flodden, op cit,* 46
13 Hall, E. *Triumphant Reigne, op cit,* 562
14 *Trewe Encountre, op cit,* 151
15 *La Rotta de Scocesi,* Roxburghe Club, 1825, 35
16 *Articles of Battle, op cit,* 2
17 Kightly, Charles *Flodden, op cit,* 47
18 Polydore, Vergil, *Historia Anglica, op cit,* book ii, 1622
19 Jones, Robert *The Battle of Flodden Field,* Edinburgh 1864, note 20
20 *Trewe Encountre, op cit,* 150
21 Hall, E. *Triumphant Reigne, op cit,* 563
22 *Articles of Battle, op cit,* 2; *Trewe Encountre, op cit,* 150
23 Hall, E. *Triumphant Reigne, op cit,* 564
24 Mackenzie, W.M. *The Secret of Flodden,* Edinburgh 1931, 92
25 Hall, E. *Triumphant Reigne, op cit,* 564
26 *Calendar of State Papers, Venice op cit,* vol ii, no 337

27 Vergil, Polydore *Historia Anglica, op cit*, vol ii, 1623
28 *Trewe Encountre, op cit*, 151

EPILOGUE

1 *Letters and Papers of Henry VIII, op cit*, vol i, no 2286
2 Jones, Robert, *Flodden Field, op cit* note 27
3 *Exchequer Rolls, op cit*, clxxxix
4 Brander, Michael *Scottish Border Battles and Ballads*, London 1976, 69
5 *Ibid*, 71
6 Scott, Sir Walter, *Poetical Works, op cit*, 56–126
7 Leslie, John *The Historie of Scotland*, Oxford, 1888, 146
8 *Notes Relative to the Fortified Walls of Edinburgh*, Edinburgh 1829
9 Cruikshank, Charles *Henry VIII and the Invasion of France*, 1994, 107
10 Barr, Niall *Flodden, op cit*, 122
11 Jones, Robert, *Flodden Field, op cit* note 27
12 Barr, Niall, *Flodden, op cit*, 120
13 *Letters and Papers of Henry VIII, op cit*, vol i, pt ii, nos 2355, 2469
14 Stowe, John *Survey of London*, 1633, 539; *Two Missions of Jacques de la Brosse*, ed. Dickinson, Gladys, Edinburgh 1942, 102
15 Head, David 'Henry VIII's Scottish Policy: A Reassessment', *Scottish Historical Review*, 1982, vol 61, 1–24
16 *Two Missions, op cit*, 102
17 Cameron, Jamie *James V*, East Linton 1998, 333
18 De la Force, Patrick *Monty's Highlanders*, Tom Donovan 1998, 117
19 Paterson, Raymond Campbell, *My Wound is Deep*, Edinburgh 1997, 215
20 Finn, Rex Welldon *Scottish Heritage*, 1938, 149
21 Devine, T.M. *The Scottish Nation 1700–2000*, Penguin 1999, 289

SELECT BIBLIOGRAPHY

Accounts of the Lord High Treasurer of Scotland, ed. James Balfour Paul and T. Dickson, 1877–1916.

Articles of Battle Account of the Battle of Flodden in Facsimiles of National Manuscripts by Sir Henry James, Director-General of the Ordnance Survey, Part 2, Southampton 1865.

Ayton, Andrew and Price, J.L. *The Medieval Military Revolution*, Tauris Academic Studies 1995.

Azar, G.A.T. *A History of Military Thought*, Oxford 2001.

Bain, J. *Calendar of Documents relating to Scotland*, Edinburgh 1881–8, 4 vols.

Baird, Ian F. *Scottish Feilde and Flodden Field: two Scottish poems*, 1982.

Barbour, John *The Bruce*, transl. George Eyre-Todd, Edinburgh 1907.

Barr, Niall *Flodden 1513*, Tempus Publishing 2001.

Barrow, G.W.S. *Robert Bruce and the Community of Scotland*, Edinburgh 1996.

Benson, Joseph *The Battle of Flodden Field (An Heroic Poem)*, Preston 1773.

Bingham, Caroline *The Voice of the Lion*, Edinburgh 1980.

Bower, Walter *Scoticronicon*, ed. and transl. D.E.R. Watt, Aberdeen 1991.

Brander, Michael *Scottish Border Battles and Ballads*, London 1975.

Brewer, J.S. *Letters and Papers in the Reign of Henry VIII*, 2 vols, 1884.

Britwell, Richard *The Closing of the Middle Ages*, Oxford 1997.

Brown, Michael *James I*, Edinburgh 1994.

Brown, Peter Hume *History of Scotland*, 3 vols, Edinburgh 1899–1909.

Brown, Thomas Craig *The Flodden Traditions of Selkirk*, Selkirk 1913.

Buchanan, George *The History of Scotland*, 3 vols, Edinburgh 1821.

Burton, John Hill *The History of Scotland*, 8 vols, Edinburgh 1897.

Caldwell, David H. *Scottish Weapons and Fortifications, 1100–1800*, Edinburgh 1981.

Cameron, Jamie *James V*, East Linton 1998.

Campbell, William *Materials for a History of the Reign of Henry VII*, 1877.

Capgrave, John *The Book of the Illustrious Henries*, ed. F. Hingeston, 1858.

Chrimes, S.B. *Henry VII*, London 1972.

Curry, Anne and Hughes, Michael (eds.) *Arms, Armies and Fortifications in the Hundred Years War*, Woodbridge 1994.

Donaldson, Gordon *Scotland James V – James VII*, Edinburgh 1990.

De La Force, *Patrick Monty's Highlanders*, Tom Donovan 1998.

Dickinson, William Croft and Pryde, George Smith *A New History of Scotland*, 1961, 2 vols.

Devine, T.M. *The Scottish Nation 1700–2000*, Penguin 1999.

Durham, Keith *The Border Reivers*, Osprey 1995.

Exchequer Rolls of Scotland ed. Stuart and Burnett, Edinburgh 1878–1908.

Featherstone, Donald *Armies and Warfare in the Pike and Shot Era 1422–1700*, 1998.

Finn, Rex Welldon *Scottish Heritage*, The Windmill Press 1938.

The Flodden Tradition, A Historical Resume: the tradition and its critics, Selkirk 1913.

The Flowers of the Forest and other songs, printed by J. and M. Robertson, Glasgow 1804.

Foeder Conventiones Literae Thomas Rymer, 3rd edn, The Hague 1739–45.

Fordun, John of *Chronicles of the Scottish Nation*, ed. W.F. Skene, Lampeter 1993.

Gairdner, James *Henry VII*, 1889.

Gibbs, Vicary (ed.) *The Complete Peerage 1910–1916*.

Grant, Alexander *Independence and Nationhood, Scotland 1306–1469*, Edinburgh 2001.

Gregory D. *The History of the Western Highlands and Isles of Scotland*, Glasgow 1881.

Hall, Edward *The Triumphant Reigne of Kyng Henry VIII*, London 1904, 2 vols. (Reprinted from the Folio edition of 1550 printed at London by Richard Galton.)

Hogg, O.F. *English Artillery 1326–1716*, 1963.

Hyland, Ann *The Warhorse*, Sutton 1998.

Jones, Archer *The Art of War in the Western World*, Oxford 1987.

Jones Robert *The Battle of Flodden Field fought September 9, 1513*, Edinburgh 1864.

Kightly, Charles *Flodden, the Anglo-Scottish War of 1513*, 1975.

Lacey, Robert *The Life and Times of Henry VIII*, 1972.

Leslie, John *The Historie of Scotland*, Oxford 1888.

Letters and Papers, foreign and Domestic, in the Reign of Henry VIII 1509–1547, ed. Brower, Gairdner and Brodie, 21 vols 1862–1910.

Linklater, Eric *The Survival of Scotland*, 1968.

MacDougall, Norman *James IV*, East Linton 1997.

Major, John *A History of Greater Britain, 1521*. ed. and transl. Archibald Constable (Scottish History Society), Edinburgh 1892.

Mackenzie, William MacKay *The Secret of Flodden*, Edinburgh 1931.

Mackie, J.D. *The Earlier Tudors 1485–1558*, Oxford 1988.

Mackie, J.D. *A History of Scotland*, Penguin Books 1991.

Mackie, J.D. (ed.) *The English Army at Flodden*, Edinburgh 1951 3rd series, vol 8.

Mackie, R.L. *King James IV of Scotland*, Edinburgh 1958.

Mackie, R.L. (ed.) *Letters of James IV 1505–1513*, Scottish History Society, Edinburgh 1953, no 543.

McGladdery, Christine *James II*, Edinburgh 1990.

McCormack, John *One Million Mercenaries, Swiss Soldiers in the Armies of the World*, 1993.

McClaren, Moray *If Freedom Fail*, 1964.

Murray, W. 'Flodden Before and After', *Transactions of the Hawick Archaeological Society*, Hawick 1913.

Nicholson, Ranald *Edward III and the Scots*, Oxford 1965.

Nicholson, Ranald *Scotland, The Later Middle Ages*, Edinburgh 1989.

Notes relative to the Fortified Walls of Edinburgh, Edinburgh 1829.

Oman, Sir Charles *A History of the Art of War in the Sixteenth Century*, London 1937.

Paterson, Raymond Campbell *For the Lion: A History of the Scottish Wars of Independence 1296–1357*, Edinburgh 1996.

Paterson, Raymond Campbell *My Wound is Deep: A History of the Later Anglo-Scottish Wars 1380–1560*, Edinburgh 1997.

Paul Sir James Balfour (ed.) *The Scots Peerage*, Edinburgh 1905, 2 vols.

Phillips, Gervase *The Anglo-Scots Wars 1513–1550*, Woodbridge 1999.

Pitscottie, Robert Lindsay of *The Historie and Chronicles of Scotland*, ed. Aeneas J.G. Mackay, Edinburgh 1899, 2 vols.

Pollard, A.F. *Henry VIII*, London 1905.

Poole, A.L. *Domesday Book to the Magna Carta 1087–1216*, Oxford 1987.

Polydore, Vergil *The Anglica Historia AD 1485–1537*. Ed. and transl. Denys Hay, Royal Historical Society 1950, Camden Series, vol 74.

Reese, Peter *The Scottish Commander*, Edinburgh 1999

Richmond, C.F. 'English Naval Power in the Fifteenth Century', *History*, vol LII, no 174 Feb 1967, 1–15.

Ridpath, Rev. George *The Border History of England and Scotland*, Berwick 1810.

Robinson, John Martin *The Dukes of Norfolk*, Chichester 1995.

Saunders, Andrew *Norham Castle*, English Heritage 1998.

Scarisbrick, J.J. *Henry VIII*, Eyre Methuen 1976.

Scott, Sir Walter *Poetical Works*, London 1869.

Scott, Sir Walter *Tales of a Grandfather*, London 1898, vol 1

Smith, Lacey Baldwin *A Tudor Tragedy, The Life and Times of Catherine Howard*, 1961.

Smith, Robert D. *Artillery and the Hundred Years War, Myth and Interpretation*.

Smith, T.B. *A Short Commentary on the Law of Scotland*, Edinburgh 1962.

Stevenson, Joseph (ed.) *Documents Illustrative of the History of Scotland* 1870, 2 vols.

Stowe John *London 1558–1603*, ed. H.B. Wheatley, Everyman Classics 1987.

Stringer, K.J. *Essays on the Nobility of Medieval Scotland*, Edinburgh 1985.

Taylor, James *The Great Historic Families of Scotland*, 1889, 2 vols.

The Trewe Encountre, written by an eyewitness, London 1513.

Tucker, M.J. *The Life of Thomas Howard, Earl of Surrey and Second Duke of Norfolk*, The Hague 1964.

Vokes, Susan Elisabeth *PhD Thesis on the early career of Thomas Howard, Third Duke of Norfolk*, Hull 1988.

Warner, Philip *British Battlefields, The North*, Osprey 1972.

Warner, Philip *Famous Scottish Battles*, Osprey 1995.

Weever, John *Ancient Funeral Monuments*, Amsterdam 1979.

Weir, Alison *Henry VIII King and Court*, London 2001.

White, John Talbot *The Death of a King, being extracts from contemporary accounts of the Battle of Branxton Moor September 1513*, Edinburgh 1970.

Wood, John Philip *The Peerage of Scotland*, Edinburgh 1813, 2 vols.

Wood, Marguerite *Diplomatic Correspondence between the Courts of France and Scotland 1507–1517, (Flodden Papers)*, Edinburgh 1933.

Index